Critical Acclaim for
Collecting Spirits

"*Collecting Spirits* covers EVERYTHING we should know about ghosts and the supernatural. It's easy to grasp and reads like a delightful conversation with a friend who shares her experiences and knowledge. One of the best books on the market today for spiritual enthusiasts!"

—Maria Shaw,
Celebrity Astrologer/Psychic Medium and Author

Collecting Spirits

BOOKS BY RENEE VALOIS

The Devil and the Diva (with David Housewright)
Collecting Spirits: Life with Ghosts, Guardians & Guides

Renee Valois

Collecting Spirits

Life with Ghosts, Guardians & Guides

Cover design by JT Lindroos

ISBN-13: 978-1-64396-396-9

TABLE OF CONTENTS

For David, my beloved partner,
and "enabler" of many wild adventures.

INTRODUCTION

Why this book?

It's a common joke that "no one gets out of here alive." We will all eventually die. But one in five Americans is afraid of death*. I wrote this book partly to alleviate their fear.

Another reason was to open people's eyes to the marvels that surround us. Many plug away at the daily grind in this "vale of tears" without noticing that there are mysteries and magic in the world. These are real, not imaginary. And the world is a much more remarkable and beautiful place when you realize that.

It's time to drop our fears and boost our awe.

*2017 "Survey of American Fears" conducted by Chapman University, 20.3% of Americans are "afraid" or "very afraid" of dying.

A Note on Belief & Disbelief

When we enter the world as babies, we know nothing. All of what we initially believe comes from another person teaching us that belief. We rely on their teaching as being the truth.

It takes time for us to see that everything we were taught may not be as true as we once assumed. Eventually we may reevaluate or change some of our beliefs based on our own direct experience and intuition.

Others hold very tightly to the views that others have taught them, as anchors that make them feel safe. They fear that if they had to give up a belief—especially about life and death—they would be cast adrift in a chaotic world, afraid and confused. They would not know where to turn, what to do, or how to live.

However, if we are open to our own authentic experiences, and don't just accept what we have been taught by others, we can find that the world is much bigger and more amazing than we had originally thought. It's not something to be feared, but to be celebrated.

There are some people who will not believe their own eyes if it contradicts what they already "know." Staunch skeptics who assert that there is no afterlife, no ghosts, no angels, no soul, will never entertain the thought that these might exist, even if a ghost appears, or a poltergeist tosses objects around the room right in front of them. They may admit that they don't know what just happened but will remain adamant that it couldn't be a ghost. Their mind is closed to any possibilities outside of their preexisting beliefs.

They will not believe it when people tell them about their paranormal experiences either—even though they originally chose to accept the word of people who told them these things do not exist.

Every living thing on this Earth evolves over time, and our beliefs and knowledge can evolve too—if we let this happen, if we are open minded.

I did not believe in ghosts for most of my life. I was always taught they were made up stories and folklore. But something happened that changed my mind.

If you read this book with an open mind, you may find your life transformed, as mine was.

* * *

A Word on Terminology

"Ghosts" are spirits of the deceased that have not gone into the light. Instead, they have decided to hang around on the Earth plane for a while, which is why they are also called "earthbound spirits." This helps differentiate them from spirits that have gone into the light or "the other side," also called "the afterlife," "heaven," "beyond the veil," and other names depending on a person's spiritual or religious beliefs.

The eternal and loving Presence at the core of all that is, may be called different things by different people, depending on their beliefs and background: God, Source, the Creator, Higher Power, the Divine, Supreme Being, Lord, the Almighty, Prime Mover, The Universe, etc. Although our understanding and relationship with this Mystery varies, I believe we all go back to the One who is our true home when we die.

I know that some people have had traumatic experiences with religion while growing up—and for them there may be baggage associated with the word "God." In that case, please simply insert your preferred alternative word (in your mind) wherever you see "God" in the text that follows.

This book does not address communicating directly with God because that relationship falls under the guidance of your specific religious beliefs. This book was created to help people of all spiritual backgrounds in their relationships with ghosts, angels and spirit guides who are not exclusive to a certain type of religion.

Naming Names

Everything in this book is accurate and exactly as I experienced it, or as other people that I trust directly told to me. However, I have changed the names of those who shared their paranormal experiences to protect their anonymity. They may have friends or relatives who would be shocked or upset by their stories, and I don't want them to suffer backlash after they trusted me enough to reveal their secrets.

If you told me of your experiences, thank you again for sharing your amazing ghostly and spiritual experiences!

EVERYTHING CHANGES

*"The visible world is an active doorway to the invisible world,
and the invisible world is much larger than the visible."*
—Richard Rohr

I was naked, lying under a thin sheet on a padded table.

Suddenly, a metal tray holding cosmetic tools flew off the counter and hit the floor with a loud crash. There was no one near it. Only I and the young woman who had been massaging me were in the room—and we were far from the counter where the tray had been resting.

It was winter and no windows were open to provide a breeze. Besides, the tray was too heavy for anything less than a gale force wind to move it.

The Laws of Physics and Gravity had just been broken.

"What the?" I asked the masseuse, "What the heck just happened? That tray!"

"Oh," she said. "That's the second or third time that has happened, always with women. I think the guys get a little excited."

"What guys?"

"This building used to be a Masonic Temple and some of the men have stuck around. The place is haunted."

When the poltergeist threw the heavy metal tray across the

room he didn't just dramatically move an object. He shifted my whole view of the world and the nature of reality.

I had never believed in ghosts.

I had always thought that they were just made-up characters created to scare and entertain us. Many Hollywood horror movies have used ghosts as fodder for the most horrific and let's face it, *ridiculous* tales.

But to witness the impossible abruptly opened my mind. I realized that the unseen world was actually real and very present. Suddenly everything became more magical and expansive. What I had thought was just fantasy was, in fact, real.

Fortunately, the unmistakable event had been witnessed by two people, so I wouldn't be left, like many solitary witnesses of inexplicable activities, to doubt my own senses or my mind, to think I might have imagined it. Also, it was concrete, physical, not just a movement caught out of the corner of my eye.

The whole thing was exciting but also reassuring—because it provided physical evidence of the existence of life after death. Atheists think we just end when our body dies, but I had seen clear indication of the contrary.

Many people are terrified by the idea of ghosts—and I suspect the ghost that threw the tray meant to frighten me. But instead I was delighted. (The joke's on him!) I'm not afraid of spirits. They're just people without bodies.

Think about it. If I threw something across a room, you might consider me rude but you wouldn't be particularly impressed. So why should you be terrified when a spirit does it? They have a lot less physical power than we do with our bodies made of matter.

Perhaps my fearlessness began in childhood when I used to watch old "Casper the Friendly Ghost" cartoons. Poor Casper was always trying to make friends with the living. Although he was a gentle, child-like spirit, people ran away in terror when they realized he was a ghost. I felt sorry for him.

I also recall a charming children's book, "Georgie", about a little ghost whose regular haunting habits helped the residents of his old house keep their lives on track.

So I didn't automatically assume ghosts are evil or harmful. They are, after all, people—much as they were in life, but invisible—which I'm sure can get frustrating for them, causing some to act out to let people know they're present.

They deserve to be treated with respect, as do all people. But they need to treat us respectfully in return. If they don't—if they cause problems—there are things we can do to remedy the situation. (See page 103 for more on this.)

When my massage was finished (minus any further interruption) and we were walking down the ornate staircase of the gorgeous old four-story building, I asked my masseuse about previous paranormal activity at the site. Apparently, a lot of the young women and men who supplied salon/spa services in the building had witnessed things.

Right then and there I decided this historic building was where I was going to head for all of my beauty and wellness needs! I hoped to have another encounter when I returned.

I drove home not merely refreshed from my massage but elated by the sudden change in my whole understanding of the world and how it operated.

Now that I had experienced something paranormal, I wanted to know if other people had experienced similar things. Was it incredibly rare? Was that why no one had ever told me they had encountered a ghost? Would they think I was crazy for bringing it up?

Probably. But I didn't care. I was dying to know more.

Forty-five percent of Americans believe that ghosts and demons exist, according to a 2019 poll of over 1,000 people. I have joined that group because of my experiences, even though I was raised Catholic. Like most Christians, Catholics are not encouraged to believe in ghosts—except for the "Holy Ghost." However, we are not told we can't believe in ghosts, either.

There were a few times in the New Testament where the apostles actually mistook Jesus for a ghost. When he walked on the water (Matthew 14:26) and when he appeared after having been crucified (Luke 24:39), they were terrified. At either point, Jesus could have set them straight by saying "Ghosts do not exist!" But he did NOT debunk ghosts. He simply told them HE was not a ghost.

I think that's rather telling.

Still, the majority of Americans do not believe in ghosts. I would guess that's because they haven't had an experience to convince them otherwise. I decided to find out just how rare such experiences are.

The poltergeist incident opened the door to the invisible world for me. I took a long look inside.

And I've never looked back.

COLLECTING GHOSTS

"The world is full of magic things,
patiently waiting for our senses to grow sharper."
—William Butler Yeats

I decided to broach the subject of ghosts with people I knew whenever there was an opportune moment. I suspected a person would be more willing to open up if I talked to them without others present. I didn't want them to fear that I might judge them or laugh at them, either.

So, I always opened the conversation by letting them know I was ready to believe their encounter by relating my own: "I once had a paranormal experience. Have you ever had anything like that happen to you?"

People who haven't had such incidents would instantly say so and often looked at me a bit oddly; I didn't bring up the subject with them again.

But I was genuinely *shocked* by how many people have indeed witnessed amazing paranormal occurrences; none of them had ever mentioned any of it to me before. In fact, the most common response I got to my question was "I've never told anyone this because I was afraid they would think I was crazy, but..." and then they would proceed to launch into the most wonderful and surprising true story.

All around us, people are encountering ghosts and spirits, but we think it's rare because everyone is afraid to talk about it. We're worried that we'll be looked at askance, sent to a psychiatrist—or worse.

It's one of our world's best-kept secrets.

Here are some of the genuine occurrences experienced by my colleagues, acquaintances, friends and relatives. These are all people I personally know and they are the last ones that a skeptic would expect to believe in ghosts. They are down-to-earth, smart, and not given to bizarre beliefs.

They had nothing to gain by making up these accounts—but they did have something to potentially lose: my respect—and their credibility. That's why most of them had not shared their experiences with anyone previously. (To be clear, I had not considered writing a book at the time, so that wasn't a factor in their disclosure one way or the other.)

I have changed their names to protect their privacy.

Stella

Stella used to share an apartment with her sister and a friend in a big old mansion that had businesses on the ground floor and apartments above them. It was located next to a well-known cemetery. Odd things would happen in that apartment.

A cheap radio Stella owned would suddenly turn on by itself—full blast. Because the sound was poor when loud, she never turned the volume up high, but it would always come on at maximum volume. Also, though she always had the radio preset to one of her favorite stations, it would turn on to some other random station, never the expected one. This happened repeatedly.

Her roommates experienced other odd things. One night, the

three of them decided to see if they could confirm whether the apartment had a ghost or not. They sat around the dining room table and closed their eyes. Stella said, "If there are any ghosts here, please give us a sign." At that moment, all five bulbs in the chandelier above their heads exploded and glass rained down on them. The light fixture's fan blades started to spin.

The three women sat there in shock, not sure what to do. They were really scared and "freaked out" as Stella described it. From that moment on, they decided not to talk about the ghosts again or to have any contact with them. They didn't plan to stay long in that apartment.

Logan

One evening, Logan saw his grandfather's face in the mirror, even though he was alone and his grandfather lived far away. The next morning, his mother called to tell him that her father had died. Logan's sister also got a visit. Their grandfather came and sat on her bed the night he died.

Years later, Logan's paternal grandfather died. Logan had a lamp—never plugged in—sitting in a guest bedroom that he didn't use. One night after his grandfather's death but before the funeral, the lamp suddenly came on—very brightly. Logan grabbed his phone to try to photograph the lamp lit up with its plug lying on the floor. But just as he took the photo, the lamp turned itself off. It was 3 am.

Another night shortly after that, Logan woke but couldn't move. As he lay there paralyzed, he saw hovering above him the shape of a person—but the shape seemed filled with electricity and he heard the sound of static. Eventually he heard the word, "Dummy", which is what his paternal grandfather always called people. Then, he saw all kinds of pictures—a lake, a forest, an old car. They were unfamiliar.

When he went to his grandfather's funeral, he saw photos of

11

the very same things and places the spirit had shown him. The old photos had been brought by his great aunts and great uncles to celebrate their brother's life.

Mia

Years ago, when Mia and her young daughter lived in a duplex built around 1900, they both received visits from a male ghost. The man came and sat on the edge of Mia's bed, wearing a cotton shirt that she thought may have been from the 1940s and a button-down coat that looked military to her. The man seemed to be about 45 or so. Mia's daughter separately received visits from the ghost in her room and described the man just as Mia saw him. He was quiet and caused them no problems.

Donald

Donald lived alone on the top floor of a duplex built in 1917. The house was at the far end of a dead-end street, close to a railroad track. One night when Donald was in bed trying to sleep, he felt something or someone push on his upper arm and elbow—but no one (that he could see) was there.

There was a lock and a deadbolt on the door—but he never used the deadbolt, just the regular lock. He would often wake up in the morning to find the deadbolt locked (from the inside), even though it hadn't been locked the night before when he went to bed.

Like many people, Donald had magnets that he kept on his refrigerator. He would wake up in the morning to find them lined up in a row on the floor beside his bed. This happened repeatedly. He began to fear his apartment was haunted.

One Sunday night shortly before Halloween, Donald was asleep in his bed when the door to his apartment slammed, waking him up. From his bedroom, he could see the shape of a man standing just inside the front door.

He sat up and rubbed his eyes, trying to see who it was. He called "Jeremy?" because his brother had been visiting him that afternoon and he thought maybe Jeremy had forgotten his cell phone and had come back for it. The man did not answer.

Suddenly the man appeared in the doorway of his bedroom. The stranger was wearing a yellow plaid shirt and was looking down at the floor, not at Donald. Adrenaline pumping, Donald leapt out of bed to confront the intruder, but the man disappeared.

Donald searched the whole apartment, but there was no sign of the man—and he had not heard or seen him exit through the outer door. He said he had seen the man's face and appearance so clearly that he could pick him out of a lineup.

Another odd thing happened shortly after that. Donald went to get a shirt out of his closet to wear to work and found that the elbow had a slit in it—the cut was clean, as if someone had cut it with a razor. There were no loose threads that would indicate it had been ripped. So Donald took out another shirt to wear instead, and that elbow also had a cut in it, in the very same spot. Donald found that three of his shirts had the same cuts in the elbow.

He did not renew his lease.

Ella

Ella studied art in college and her Mom bragged about her talent to a customer at her framing shop. The man arranged for Ella and her roommate to each paint his portrait. He would come to their apartment for sittings in full regalia, wearing a long elaborate robe, claiming he was a Warlock.

Between sittings, the two paintings-in-progress sat on their apartment table and the Warlock's painted eyes seemed to be staring at the two women. It bothered them, so they covered up the unfinished paintings.

But several times in the morning when they awoke, the cloths that covered the paintings had been removed, and the Warlock was staring directly at them from the paintings.

They decided to set the paintings on the floor and turn them to face the wall, with shoes propped at the bases, so the canvases couldn't fall over. In the morning they would find the portraits facing outward, with the Warlock's eyes again locked on them.

Each accused the other of turning the paintings, but both denied it. Eventually they asked the Warlock if he were doing it. He said no—but said they definitely had ghosts in their apartment who WERE moving the paintings.

Ruby & Lydia

I stayed overnight with Ruby in a house that belonged to her mother Lydia's longtime partner. It had been his parents' home (built in 1962) and I sensed they might still be there. When I suggested there might be spirits in the home, Lydia confirmed that yes, there were.

She and her partner slept in the basement even though there were two nice bedrooms upstairs. I slept in the bedroom that had belonged to his parents and felt a presence (not threatening). I was told that the presence was the owner's mother, who had passed away in the house of a heart attack.

Doors in that house left open would often close by themselves, and sounds could be heard coming from the kitchen in the middle of the night when no one was there.

I also learned that Lydia, Ruby and her brother had lived in several haunted houses through the years. Two of the houses had been empty for a while and they bought the houses cheaply. They soon learned the bargain prices may have been due to paranormal activity.

At one house, things kept disappearing and they'd never be able to find them again.

If they set an item down and looked away for a second, it would be gone before they looked back.

Shortly before they finally left that house, they removed a shelf bolted to the wall. Behind it they found a wooden panel that was screwed shut. Curious about what the panel concealed, Ruby removed it. There, covered in cobwebs and dust, were all of the things that had gone missing while they lived in the house, as well as some much older items that weren't theirs. Everything had the same thick layer of dust on it as if all of the items had been put there at the same time.

In the next house, Ruby's brother kept getting locked in his bedroom. They never locked his door because it required a skeleton key which they didn't have. But when he would get up in the morning, the door would be locked and he couldn't leave. He began keeping the tools he needed to pick the lock in his bedroom so he could get out.

They had a number of ghosts in that house, but the only one they actually saw was that of a little girl who rode her tricycle around the basement. They would also find children's toys scattered in the basement that weren't theirs. The ghost girl would slam doors if they put the toys away. So they created a small "play area" in one corner of the basement for her.

In a different house early in Lydia's first marriage, they would often come home to the smell of baking bread, with all of the lights on and music playing, even though nothing had been on when they left.

They also received numerous complaints about noise from their neighbors when they were out of town for the night. The neighbors said that they could see figures dancing through drawn curtains as loud music played. They even called the police about the loud parties. But when the officers arrived, they found no vehicles in the driveway, no lights on, and no music playing.

When the couple decided to sell that house, the ghost tried to keep them from leaving. Every time their Realtor would show the place to a prospective buyer, everything would go wrong. Closet doors wouldn't open, the lights wouldn't work, there would be no hot water, etc. But as soon as the agent left, everything worked fine.

The woman who died in that house was the elderly sister of the next-door neighbor.

They learned that she had died suddenly while home alone making bread. She had tried to call 911 but passed before help arrived.

To bring her closure, they baked bread in the house and had a picnic with the sister in the cemetery by the woman's headstone. After that, they had less activity in the home. They eventually were able to sell it.

Chrissy

Chrissy worked for a while at a high-end spa in a huge old house. When she was there alone, working on the books after hours, doors would suddenly slam shut. More disturbingly, she would hear the sounds of partying—footsteps, voices, music, glasses clinking—that sounded like they were coming from upstairs. But there was no floor above her. During the day, sometimes customers would hear the sounds of the partying above them and ask if there was another floor. Since there was not, that made for a rather awkward conversation.

Vanessa

When Vanessa was in high school, she agreed to give a ride home to one of her younger teammates after athletic practice.

She asked the girl where she lived. Her teammate said she lived in a house across the street from the elementary school, but she wasn't sure how much longer they'd be living there. Vanessa asked why and the girl told her that her father travelled a lot, and whenever he was gone, a woman would come and stand at the foot of her mother's bed.

When they arrived at the house, Vanessa was quite surprised. She said, "This is my aunt and uncle's old house. My uncle built it." Then she asked the girl if her mother's bedroom was on the first floor in a particular back corner of the house. The girl said yes, how did she know that? Vanessa said that's where her aunt had died, alone—because at that time she and her husband were separated.

I said I hoped she told the girl that her aunt wasn't going to hurt her mother or cause any harm and she said, yes, she told the girl her aunt was harmless although she might show up with a cigarette dangling from her mouth (since she smoked non-stop).

She never learned if they moved or not.

Sam

Sam lived in an apartment by himself. But he would walk into the kitchen and find all of the cabinet doors open when they had been closed minutes before. This happened over and over.

Finally, one day, he said loudly, "It would really be great if the kitchen cabinet doors quit opening up all the time." He had no trouble with them after that.

(Fortunately, ghosts often do listen to the living and can take a hint, as I've found out myself.)

Vanessa 2

Eventually, Vanessa told me of the experience that changed her mind about ghosts; at the time neither she nor her husband believed in them. They had planned a weekend trip with another couple to Duluth and made reservations for both couples to share a room at a historic Inn on Lake Superior. When the other couple found out where they were staying, the man protested. He said he didn't want to stay at the Inn because it was haunted.

Vanessa's husband made fun of that reaction. He said there were no such things as ghosts and told the other guy to "man up." Both couples eventually did end up sharing a large room at the Inn with two double beds and a raised area near the window with a table and chairs.

Vanessa said that they all went to sleep fine, but her husband woke up in the middle of the night. He was shocked to see a dark figure walking from one end of the raised area to the other—and then back again. He woke Vanessa and she also saw the shadow figure passing back and forth. They couldn't sleep for the rest of the night.

Both she and her husband now believe in ghosts—and they won't go back to that Inn. In the morning, they told the guy who was afraid of ghosts that they now believed him—and why.

Naomi

Naomi used to work for an ad agency that was housed in an old brownstone with a turret right across from a Women's Club bordering a popular city park. She said that they had started renovating the building, but hadn't done much yet on the third floor, which housed her office. The only other room on that floor was for storage and it had a latched handle you had to turn to open the door.

One day Naomi saw the handle turn all by itself, and the

door opened. But there was no one else there. In addition to doors opening and closing by themselves, people were always having problems with things disappearing and reappearing in the office.

A designer was working late one night, alone in the building. He had just finished up an important project and left the papers on his desk before stepping away to get something. When he returned, the papers were gone. He said, "Are you kidding me?" threw up his hands, and left.

When he returned the next morning, the papers were back on his desk.

Naomi said an old man showed up one day and asked if he could look around the place. He said he had lived there as a child with his mother. It turned out the building had been a "War Widows Home" for women and children of men serving in the war (probably WWI, given the man's age many years ago).

The man asked Naomi if they had seen "her" and she said yes—although up until that point, they'd had no idea if the ghost was a man or woman. The man said that the house had been haunted when he had stayed there many years earlier; the ghost was of a little girl from the nineteenth century.

Naomi told him about the door handle turning on the third floor and he said that room had been the girl's bedroom. That gave Naomi a chill.

I wondered why the girl had stuck around instead of moving on and Naomi said that her room still had the original wallpaper and flooring, although it was not in great shape. Most of the house had been renovated, but her bedroom had not, so maybe it still felt like home to the little ghost girl.

Mack

Mack lived in a haunted house when he was a kid. Shortly after they moved in, his mom saw a man wearing a black suit and a top hat standing at the foot of her bed. She tried to wake her husband, but the man disappeared. They later learned that the previous owner, who died in the house, always wore top hats.

Mack often heard footsteps coming up the stairs late at night when there was no one else home. When he went to take a look, there was never anyone there. He also saw doors close by themselves when there was no wind, no windows open—and no reason at all for the doors to move.

He had many nightmares in the house, all focused on the closet in his room.

Eventually his mother had a priest come and bless the house and the activity stopped.

Daniel

When Daniel was young, he used to visit a friend whose parents had bought an old Victorian mansion built by the owner of one of the many German breweries that used to exist in that small town.

While Daniel and his buddy were alone in the house, watching TV upstairs, they would hear the chairs in the kitchen moving around. When they went down to see what was going on, they found the chairs all tossed about, and no one else at home. Lights would also flicker on and off and doors would open and close on their own.

Once, his friend's mom seemed to be talking to someone as she stood on a ladder. She said, "I won't." But they were the only ones with her and hadn't said anything. They asked her what she meant. It turned out that she had felt someone steady her ladder and say, "Don't fall." She had responded to that.

Daniel said that the brewery owner had supposedly murdered his wife and then killed himself in the basement, and a lot of people didn't like going down there. It felt "wrong," But there was a gigantic wine cellar in the basement and he and his friend would take the hinges off the padlocked door (which he said were on the wrong side, so they could just pop the pins) and raid it for fine bottles of wine to take to parties. Years later, they came clean to the parents about all those missing bottles—it wasn't the ghosts' fault!

Daniel also said his most remarkable ghost experience was actually with his father. Their rule was to never part without saying goodbye. But his Dad died and didn't get to say goodbye to Daniel.

However, a day or so after his father died, Daniel was in bed when he heard a loud tick that sounded like a clock—except it was super loud. Then he felt a painful pressure in his chest and he wondered if he was having a heart attack. There was a huge whoosh and suddenly his dad was standing there. He felt as if his father was saying goodbye.

This had a huge impact on Daniel. He said he couldn't even describe the feeling. It was wonderful.

Patsy

When I was on the phone with my mother-in-law and mentioned I was watching a TV show about people's paranormal experiences, she said her grandmother regularly saw ghosts in the house they lived in during the 1940s.

Her grandmother would calmly mention that she saw a lady in white standing by the window in the dining room or the front room. Patsy and her siblings weren't afraid because their grandmother wasn't.

They never saw the ghost—in a reversal of the usual situation where kids see the ghost and the adults do not. My husband was shocked to learn of the ghost because his mother had never mentioned it to him or his brothers.

Corrine & Roger

Corrine and Roger live in a gorgeous old mansion where they have experienced a variety of paranormal activity. Roger's son has seen a woman's apparition, and his bedroom has an "off" feel to it. Things are always disappearing, only to show up later in odd places. Doors open and shut by themselves.

Corrine interviewed a psychic for a magazine article she was writing when the woman, out of the blue, told Corrine that she had ghosts in her house. She said that there were two children, and they loved Corrine's house because there were toys in practically every room.

The psychic also told Corrine that her daughter was going to have a baby boy—before Corrine even knew that her daughter was pregnant. Sure enough, she now has a grandson.

Josie

One neighbor said that when she was a university student, her apartment was haunted. Doors would open and close by themselves. She always had a bad feeling about the area where she slept. One night, her dresser started shaking so violently, it really scared her. There was no traffic, construction nearby or anything to cause it.

She moved out of that apartment as soon as she could.

Carter

Carter grew up in a haunted house, but that didn't deter him from buying it. When his parents downsized, he and his wife moved into the home his grandparents had built, situated on a beautiful city creek.

He said that when he was a kid, his mother would hear footsteps at night when she was in bed and think one of her six kids had gotten up. The bathroom door would close and the light would come on. But after a while, when the door remained closed, his mom would wonder if the child in the bathroom were ill and she would go to see what was wrong. When she opened the door, the light was on, but no one was there.

Carter moved into the basement bedroom when his older brother moved out. He often heard footsteps coming down the stairs, but when he looked out, he saw no one.

There was a lot of other activity. But it all stopped when his sister moved out. That's when they figured out that the ghost was attached to HER, not the house. She eventually told the ghost that it scared her and to go away—and it did. So the house was quiet when Carter and his wife bought it.

Eliza

Eliza was in the basement of an antique shop when she felt something on her arm. Little bits of glass were falling on her sleeve and rolling down her arm onto the floor. This happened repeatedly. She looked up at the ceiling to see where the glass was coming from but saw no source for it. She had an odd feeling and looked around.

Suddenly a sachet, a small cloth bag filled with potpourri, flew out of a basket sitting on top of an antique dresser and landed on the floor. Another one flew out of the basket. Then another.

Eliza went upstairs to ask the shop owner if anything odd had ever happened in the basement. He asked her where she had been standing and what she had seen. When she described her experience, he was quite dismayed. He said he thought they had gotten rid of the ghost when they sold an antique bed—but it must instead be attached to the matching dresser, which they hadn't yet sold.

Jean

Jean's two young daughters both saw entities in their relatively new house. One daughter was frightened to sleep in her room because she saw a "cowboy and a farmer" who were fighting with each other. The ghosts wanted her to help them. She was scared and didn't know what to do.

Jean told her to tell them that she was just a kid and couldn't help them—that they needed to go ask an adult. That seemed to help.

The land where the house was situated had once been a farm that included horses, so that could be why Jean's daughter was seeing what appeared to be a farmer and a cowboy.

Her other daughter also saw a person in her parents' dark and empty room one night. Jean asked her to draw what she saw and the girl drew a half figure, with legs and part of a body. There was no head or upper body; her daughter had seen a partial apparition.

One daughter saw faces in various rooms in the house. Some looked happy but others looked darker. Jean decided to bring in an expert to clear the house. She also smudged the home (burning herbs meant to discourage ghosts) whenever the energy felt heavier. Activity seemed to wane as the girls got older.

Jean also had an experience after her beloved dog died at age 15. She thought she heard the dog's collar jingling but discounted that as wishful thinking. However, one day she walked into her bedroom to find little pawprints all over the bed, just like her dog used to make. The family owned no animals at the time. In fact, they had been so devastated by their dog's death that they did not get another dog for eight years. Jean was freaked out by the ghostly pawprints and grabbed the blanket to shake it out.

When she was younger, Jean had received comforting visits from her grandparents after they had passed. She wasn't sure if she was awake or if she had received vivid dream visitations from them.

Her grandmother was so radiant and luminous that Jean exclaimed how beautiful she was.

Her grandfather came separately, accompanied by a horse and a dog. All three of them looked transparent and sparkled. Jean's grandfather had owned horses, so that was not surprising, and he had always talked about a beloved dog he had owned. They were clearly with him in the afterlife.

Diane & Annie

Diane was a real estate agent doing a walk-through at a house an elderly lady planned to sell. The woman told her that her deceased husband sometimes made his presence known.

Afterwards, Diane and her daughter Annie stood outside the house, facing a tall pine tree in the front yard, while talking with the owner. Suddenly, one of the large branches of the tree bent way, way down toward the ground as if someone were pulling it downward. Then the branch sprang back up wildly as if it had just been released. Diane and Annie stared at each other in amazement. There was no rational explanation for the extreme movement of that one branch. They suspected that the husband was indeed letting them know he was still there.

Violet

Violet was only three years old when her father (a deputy sheriff) was killed at age 32. Her parents had been high school sweethearts who married soon after graduation and had three young children.

Violet couldn't understand where her dad had gone and kept looking for him. Her Mom, Lily, was grief-stricken but would never cry in front of the children. She tried to put on a calm face.

But after she had put the three children to sleep for the night, Lily would cry alone in her bed, grieving the loss of her husband, worrying about the family's future—and fearing that Matt may have suffered terribly during his death.

One night, the bedroom light came on and she saw her handsome husband standing there. Matt walked over to the bed and sat down on it. He reassured Lily that he was okay and didn't want her grieving over him. Everything was going to be okay. Then he said he had to go.

Lily begged him to stay but he said he could not. He stood up and left.

After he disappeared, she wondered if it had just been a dream. But then she saw the impression on the bed where he had been sitting—and the light was on, even though she had turned it off when she went to bed.

On a later date, Lily was trying to even out dirt in the garden with a rake and couldn't get it smooth the way her husband used to do so well. She said, "Oh, Matt, how did you used to do this? I don't know how you did it!"

Suddenly, the rake handle turned around by itself in her hands, and she realized that he used the back of the rake to smooth the dirt, not the pronged side.

Matt appeared again to his beloved—after she had married a good friend of his, a kind man who had been a bachelor. Lily looked down the hallway of her new home to see Matt standing there, grinning at her. She felt it was a signal of approval and also "goodbye." Everything had indeed turned out fine as he had said it would. She never saw him again.

As an adult, Violet had an experience of her dad through a medium. A mentor and friend recommended she see a respected psychic who was coming into town. Violet and her husband went but were very skeptical.

As the psychic walked down the line of attendees, telling each person a thing or two about their loved ones, the people she addressed appeared amazed by her comments. Violet and her husband said "Yeah, right!" to each other, quietly making fun of the proceedings.

Then the psychic reached Violet. "Matthias is with you," she said. "He is often around you." Violet felt a sudden shock and got goosebumps. Everyone had called her father "Matt" and most people assumed his name was "Matthew" since "Matt" was usually the shortened form of that name. But her dad's name was actually "Matthias," an uncommon name.

The psychic was spot on.

Luke

When he was in the military in Southeast Asia, Luke took a trip while on leave, traveling as a civilian. The first leg of the itinerary led from Saigon to Singapore. No one he met knew that he was in the military. His nickname at that time was Rusty, as it had been in high school. No one knew his real name.

An Australian woman he met on his flight soon introduced him to other people. One night they were partying in the Puay Hee district and someone suggested they play "Spirit of the Glass." They set a cocktail glass upside down on the table with scraps of paper handwritten with letters, numbers, "yes," and "no," like on a Ouija board.

Then they placed their fingertips lightly on the glass and asked if the spirits had a message. They got a "yes." They asked who the message was for and got "Luke". No one knew who that was (except Luke). They asked who the message was from. The name that came up was someone Luke knew who had been killed in action in Vietnam. The message was, "Be careful out there."

Wyatt

Wyatt has an interest in the paranormal and specifically went to the Palmer House in Sauk Center because he had heard it was haunted. The hotel was built in 1900 on the site of an earlier hotel that had burned down.

While Wyatt and his wife were enjoying a drink in the bar, they saw a glass fly off an empty table and smash into the wall. No one was near it.

I was jealous. When David and I had gone to the Palmer House, even though we'd stayed in one of the rooms that supposedly had a lot of paranormal activity, nothing had happened.

The only things we *had* seen were two EMF meters lighting up to the maximum when the owner of the hotel brought out the dress of the woman who had run the hotel in its early days—it was the same gorgeous dress she was wearing in her portrait hanging on the wall.

The owner said that the woman was right there with us in the lobby.

David

My husband had the sad duty of attending a funeral for a former schoolmate, a woman who had died far too early. He was standing in a pew with fellow classmates when suddenly, in the middle of the service, someone pinched him on the butt.

He quickly looked around to identify the culprit. There was no one near him on the side where his cheek had been pinched, and no sign of movement from the people next to him on his other side. They were still solemnly looking forward, their hands in view. None of them seemed like the type that would do something so irreverent in the middle of a funeral, either.

Later, David realized that the pinch was exactly the kind of thing that his newly deceased friend would have done.

She had let him know, in her telltale "cheeky" way, that she was still around and just fine.

Dee & Ann

When she was young, Dee's daughter Ann would often wake in the middle of the night. She would then head to her parents' bedroom for comfort, and either lie on the floor next to their bed or climb in beside her mother.

Once, Dee and Ann both woke in the darkness. Down the hallway they saw a billowy, floating figure. It looked like a woman in a flowing gown with full sleeves, like a choir robe. They could make out long hair and the shape of a face, but the features weren't clear. The white apparition did not appear completely solid, reminding Dee of sheer gauze. After a few moments, it disappeared.

Dee and Ann were not frightened because the figure did not seem threatening. Ann felt that the figure was maternal and even comforting. Dee wondered if their visitor had been checking on the children.

They never saw the spirit again.

Tom

My brother had a paranormal experience in his first house many years ago. He went down into the basement where double cement washtubs stood at the foot of the stairs. Overhead was a fluorescent light fixture, which usually held a long bulb that illuminated both laundry tubs.

On this one day, though, one end of the fluorescent bulb sat on the floor while the opposite end rested on the front of the cement tubs.

Tom asked his wife if she had removed the bulb, and she said no. She knew nothing about it. Their children were very small and couldn't reach the fixture attached to the ceiling.

Tom could not figure out a rational way the bulb could have ended up where it did. If the bulb had fallen out of its bracket, it would have smashed into the cement tubs below and broken. Even if it had miraculously remained intact, it couldn't have landed outside the tubs at a ninety-degree angle.

The bulb's position appeared deliberately placed. But no one living in the house had done it.

* * *

Through friends, the internet, newspapers and books, I learned about supposedly haunted locations within driving distance and decided to visit some of them.

Billy's Bar & Grill

Billy's Bar & Grill is on the first floor of a three-story red brick building built in the late 19th century as a hotel. Now the upper stories are just used for storage. I had read that Billy's was haunted, so we went there for supper at Happy Hour (well worth it!)

When I asked our cheerful young waitress about the rumored haunting, she sent me to see the pony-tailed bartender in the bar area. He seemed reluctant to talk and put me off with, "Later."

When I returned later, he agreed to talk. He said that right before he left the bar at night, he would always turn off the many TV's that were mounted up on the walls of the bar and restaurant areas.

But when he switched off one television and went to do

another, the first TV would come back on. He'd shut off the power again and when he turned around, the television would be back on. This would happen repeatedly when he was alone. But if someone else walked in and he said "watch this," and turned off the TV, it would stay off. He said the ghost's game was over if there were other witnesses.

The bartender said the historic framed photos on the walls would often tilt sideways, even when there was no one there, and no vibrations of any kind to cause the shift. That happened a lot. They constantly had to straighten the pictures.

He had heard voices as well; he thought the ghost was female, but the words were garbled so he couldn't make out what she was saying. Lights would flip back on after they were turned off—or go dark after he had turned them on.

After some such spooky goings on in the basement, he stayed away from that area for a while. Finally, he went back down one evening and turned on all the lights to see what might happen. When nothing occurred, he made a little disgusted "hmmph!" noise and turned to leave. That's when the door slammed shut loudly. He said there was no breeze or other explanation for the sudden, forceful slam—and he got out of there fast.

He directed me to the manager, Melina, who said she had also had odd experiences with the televisions. When the remote control for all the TVs was broken, she had to climb up on the table to turn off one in the corner and when she got down, it came back on. This happened with several of the televisions she tried to turn off.

She also said a long-time employee (the sister of the woman standing next to her—who immediately confirmed the incident) had gone upstairs to get some glasses in the storage area. They asked her to change the channel on the radio station that piped music throughout the building while she was up there.

The woman found the box of glasses she had come for, put them on the floor, and reached over to change the channel on the radio. The controls were very dusty, and she left a visible handprint on top of the console,

Then she turned to pick up her load of glasses and when she glanced back, there was a whole pyramid of glasses stacked on top of her handprint on the radio—which hadn't been there just a second before.

Gibbs Museum

The Gibbs Museum includes several buildings: an 1850s era house, a nineteenth-century one-room schoolhouse, old barns, and reproductions of a sod house. There are also a Dakota bark lodge, tipis, and camps. The house (just down the street from where I live) has had a lot of activity over the years.

Volunteer docents have told me that they have felt tugging and movement of their period-appropriate skirts in the house when there was no breeze or window open. Even visiting kids have pointed out the odd movement of the skirts. Doors open and close by themselves. Footsteps sound upstairs when no one is there.

In the house, Mrs. Gibb's bedroom has a very fragile antique handmade rug and the room is roped off to protect it and the room's furnishings from visitors. The draperies are normally closed to protect the bedding, rug and upholstery from sunlight. But the manager arrived in the morning when nobody had been there to find that the curtains had all been opened wide and sunlight was streaming in.

Toys kept in a locked cabinet have also been found strewn around the floor in the morning as if someone had been playing with them.

Museum Mansion

Many hotels, restaurants, museums, and businesses do NOT want people to know that their location is haunted because they fear it will deter visitors and lead to a drop in income. One such place is a historic mansion that we visited on Lake Superior. My husband and I took a nighttime flashlight tour of the beautiful home.

When I asked our two young female tour guides if the place was haunted, they assured us that they don't publicize the house as such. However, when pressed later in private, one of them said that when she was alone in the house at Christmastime, she saw a shadow in the shape of a human figure pass right between her and the lit Christmas tree. People have also heard footsteps when no one else was there.

She said there had been more activity since some new items were added to the sewing room, especially in the portion of the house near that room, so they thought a ghost might have come in with some of the recently acquired antique items on display there.

Water Street Inn

We had a lovely dinner and stayed overnight at a historic hotel along a river. Of course, I asked the person who manned the front desk if they had experienced any paranormal activity. He admitted that there was a room on the third floor that one of their longtime housekeepers refused to clean because of paranormal experiences she had had there.

He also said a number of their housekeepers had seen a woman dressed in old-time red clothing on the third floor—but oddly enough, not in the part of the hotel built in 1890, but in the newer section that was once the site of a grocery store.

It's possible the woman may have come in with some of the beautiful Victorian furniture that fills the rooms, since ghosts are known to attach themselves to things, as well as people and places.

The man said that the weekend before, a corporation had rented the entire hotel. The employees had been singing and playing the grand piano in the lobby, partying and having a good time. They shut the piano cover over the keys when they all left to go to an event. About five minutes later, he and a coworker heard the loud plunk of a single piano key, even though the cover was still closed.

The man said that he had suggested doing a ghost tour to the owners, but they didn't want to publicize the fact that the hotel may be haunted. They were afraid ghosts might keep some people away.

Unfortunately, we did not experience anything while staying overnight there.

American Swedish Institute

We attended a Halloween Bash at a historic Nordic mansion and I spoke to the case manager of a ghost hunters group that had investigated the place. He said when they had asked if anyone was present, they received a clear "yes" EVP (electric voice phenomenon) on their digital recorder. None of them had heard the response with their ears at the time, but the recorder captured it.

Later, they caught two voices speaking in a foreign language—and were hoping the staff at the mansion could determine if the language was Swedish, since the people who built the home were from Sweden.

The ghost hunter also said that when he was sitting in the room next to where we were standing, the door opened on its own. The investigative team tried to reproduce this action but couldn't get the door to move without help, no matter what method they tried.

I asked him to name the most haunted site they had investigated. He said the Palmer House in Sauk Center. When they get new members, they always take them there because it's guaranteed something paranormal will happen. It's very "active" (which is the word they prefer instead of "haunted.").

He also said the Soap Factory basement is very active and has a negative energy. When you go into the basement it's dark, but the darkness gets even blacker. He said it's hard to explain, but you can feel it. A lot of animals were killed and rendered there when their fat was used to create soap. They couldn't talk about some of their investigations because the people involved have asked them to keep it private.

I later learned that one of those secret investigations was at the Masonic Temple where I had first learned that ghosts are real.

BACK TO THE
TEMPLE OF GHOSTS

*"I would rather have a mind opened by wonder
than one closed by belief."*
—Gerry Spence

As I mentioned earlier, I decided to return as often as I could to the haunted former Masonic Temple where a poltergeist crashed my world. My next opportunity to go back was when the salon/spa held a fundraising event for a clean water charity. I attended, bought some items—and sidled over to the serious-looking, uniformed security guard standing against the wall. I asked her if she had ever experienced anything paranormal in the building.

She looked me in the eye, nodded, and said that at night when she was there alone making her rounds, she'd walk by the elevator and the doors would suddenly open with no one inside. She'd head up to the second floor and just as she walked by the elevator, again the doors would abruptly open and there would be no one visible. She'd go to the third floor and as she walked by the elevator—you guessed it, same eerie thing. She said the elevator doors always opened at the exact moment she walked by, and it always appeared empty.

Then she added, "Of course, this is where they brought all the bodies." I said, "What? What bodies?" At that very moment, she received an urgent call, said "I have to go," and immediately left.

I watched for her return but never saw her again. The comment about the bodies haunted me. I was determined to learn more.

Months later, I struck up a conversation with two women who had worked in the building. One said that people would hear voices—including that of a little girl—when there was no one else present. She claimed there was a particularly nasty ghost in the basement and that area was the main focus of activity; several people had felt someone try to push them down the stairs when no one else was there.

Her companion said that while she was there late one night doing paperwork, doors opened and closed by themselves. The fire alarm went off—but they found no sign of smoke or anything that would have triggered it.

She also said there used to be a crematorium in the basement, and there were trap doors and a tunnel that led under the pavement to a smaller building across the street which had been a mortuary. She thought they had transported bodies through the tunnel from the mortuary to the crematorium.

A crematorium is a structure in which dead bodies are burned at very high temperatures (1400-2000 degrees) until all that remains are brittle bones. These are then crushed into tiny bits referred to as "ashes".

When I learned about the crematorium in the basement of the Masonic Temple, all of the activity in the building suddenly made sense. It wasn't only the Masons who were probably hanging around.

Who knows how many hundreds of dead souls may have come through the building while their bodies were being cremated and then decided to hang around for a while? It was a beautiful building, after all, in a busy area of the city. All the living people there could provide entertainment—and energy—for the earthbound spirits.

Caleb

Caleb told me that he had actually experienced more activity at his office across the street in the former mortuary than in the old Masonic Temple, especially when he was there alone at night.

One night all of the doors in the single-story building simultaneously opened and then shut—over and over and over. He decided that meant the ghosts were bored—and also that maybe he should head home.

Sienna

When I went back to the salon to get my roots colored, I had a new young stylist. When I asked her my usual question about paranormal experiences, Sienna shouted, "Yes!" She said she went to a presentation in one of the big rooms in the building. There were a bunch of chairs set up, but not many people were present, so they only used the chairs near the front of the room. Suddenly, a chair in the back lifted up and went flying across the room, crashing sideways into the wall—although no one was anywhere near it. "We were all freaked out!" she said.

She added that once, she used her comb on a customer at her station and put it down on the counter. When she reached for it again, it wasn't there. In fact, she couldn't find it anywhere. She thought, "Am I going crazy?"

Finally, she gave up and stepped away to get a new comb—and when she returned, her comb was sitting right there on the counter where she thought she had originally left it. She said this had happened several times. It was like they were messing with her.

Lissa

A year later, I went to another young stylist at the salon who suggested that I get a massage there. When I told her the story of my original massage with a side of paranormal activity, she told me something very strange had happened in the building that she couldn't explain.

A man had been causing such a disturbance in the lobby, they had called the building's security guards—and the police. Two security guards escorted the man out of the building and he immediately took off. I asked what he looked like and she said he was tall and wearing a suit.

When the police finally arrived, they asked to look at video footage from the security cameras, because they thought they might be able to identify the man. But when everyone looked at the footage, they saw the security guards heading toward the door and it looked like they were holding onto someone, but there was NO ONE there. They could see the eyes of the people sitting in the lobby watching the guards escort the invisible person to the door, but the guards' hands were holding NOTHING. Obviously, the police couldn't identify the invisible man.

Lissa said she wasn't there when the incident happened, but a group of them later looked at the video, and it was freaky.

Can ghosts temporarily make themselves solid or was something else going on with the "invisible man"? I'm not sure what to make of this incident, but I'm not terribly surprised that it happened at what I think of as the "Temple of Ghosts."

Melanie

I had to change my appointment date, and my usual stylist was not available. So. when I went in, I had the opportunity to ask a new person about paranormal activity.

Melanie knew something of the building's history. She said after it was a Masonic Temple, it was a department store. Eventually it became an events venue, and the theater upstairs hosted up-and-comers such as Jimi Hendrix.

I asked her if there had indeed been a crematorium onsite as I'd heard and she said "Yes, and it's still in the basement!" In addition to the funeral home across the street, she said there were all kinds of tunnels in the area, connecting the church to the funeral home, which was connected to the building we were in.

As far as activity in the old Masonic Temple, she said people were always getting touched and poked when they were alone—and when they looked around, there was no one there.

Also, she said the toilets have motion sensors that make them flush, but they keep flushing by themselves when no one's near them. The management has had them checked several times, and they keep getting told by the technicians that there's nothing wrong with the sensors. Yet, the toilets keep flushing. One woman heard a girl call "Mommy" in the bathroom when no one else was there.

One day, when Melanie was in a back room, the lid suddenly flew off the trash can. A friend standing in the doorway saw it too and he said, "Well, let's analyze this. There was nothing in the trash can and nothing near it that would cause that..." Neither of them could explain it by normal means.

Melanie said there was more activity upstairs than on the first floor where we were. She said "shadow people" were often spotted there—especially by the security guards. Some of the guards had made "friends" with the paranormal denizens of the building and actually talked to them out loud as they were making their rounds.

* * *

Georgina and Margie

A new stylist who colored my hair said she loved old houses and antiques—as I do—and we discovered we had a lot in common. But she was moving in two weeks, so I wouldn't see her again.

Georgina said that when she was on the second floor in the old nail area, getting ready to do a pedicure, someone put a hand on her back and she turned around, thinking a friend wanted her attention. But there was no one there. When her friend actually came into the room, Georgina said, "Please tell me you touched my back, then walked out and came back in." Her friend said, no, she had not done that. In fact, someone had touched her back, too, and she'd thought it had been Georgina.

Georgina said most people seem to have experiences there when they're alone.

She also said her family had experienced paranormal things at their house. But her Mom told her the ghost was harmless, like Casper, so it didn't bother her. The spirit just turned lights off and on and moved objects around.

When a veteran stylist was helping to detangle my long curly hair after it had been colored and shampooed, I asked her if she had any paranormal experiences in the building and she said, "So many!"

Margie said she had been working in the building for 30 years. She knew and worked with the founder of the business, who had died years earlier. He had loved jasmine, and she sometimes smelled it out of the blue. She thought he was present and might help to calm some of the more negative spirits.

I asked why some of the spirits were negative. Margie thought some of the men from the days when the building was a Masonic Temple were unhappy there were so many women around now.

She said the third through fifth floors were the most active. A paranormal investigative group had come into the building a few years earlier and they wanted people who had been there for a long time to take part in their investigation. Margie said that she and a longtime coworker stayed overnight from 10 pm to 4 am with the group. They split into smaller groups and stayed for a while in each area of the building. A lot of things happened.

Margie said she's a Sensitive, and when she was in the fifth floor's Crystal Room, she had a vision of a young girl in a 1900s dress with a lollipop and long hair. The psychic who was with her asked, "Is there a young girl here?" because she got a similar sense. She thinks it's the spirit of a girl who lived in the area before the Masonic Temple was built. Margie said she also heard calliope music in the room, as did the psychic—but no one else with them heard it.

At one point, Margie said she felt ill and was heading toward the bathroom when she heard a voice say "Bitch!" It showed up on their recording equipment as an EVP, but she said she heard the insult more loudly in person than it sounded on the recording. They got lots of EVPs that night. I asked if the ghostly EVPs were mostly positive or negative. She said they got both, but more negative EVPs.

She doesn't like to be there alone at night.

Margie said she was dead tired after the investigation and went home to bed about 4:30 am. When she woke, a picture in her bedroom that had been there for years was tilted sideways on the wall—something that had never happened before. She felt that someone had followed her home from the building, which freaked her out. So she called her professional psychic friend to come and help her with super-strength sage to clean out her place.

Margie asked if I had ever seen the Crystal Room (where she and the psychic sensed the ghost girl) and I said no, so she told Georgina to take me up to see it.

The room was small, about the size of a bedroom and there was a soaring dome overhead with a multi-point quartz crystal in its center. There was also light shining through smaller crystals set into the ceiling surrounding it. It was beautiful and unusual. I could see why ghosts might want to hang out there.

* * *

Faith

By the time I returned to the Masonic Temple for another color touch-up, Georgina had moved on, so I met Faith. She had bright red and blue hair and admitted that she didn't know that the building was haunted before she arrived.

She said that she was alone after hours in the basement when she heard a loud knocking that seemed to be coming from the vicinity of the closed door. When it happened again, she went to the door and opened it, thinking someone may have gotten locked out (the door would sometimes automatically lock when you shut it), but saw no one. It happened several more times, creeping her out—especially since she was alone. She decided to get out of there.

Faith also mentioned the toilets flushing repeatedly (as Melanie had). She said they had motion sensors that seemed to sense something that no one could see. She said everyone who had been there for any length of time had lots of stories.

Faith believed a studio in the basement was the most haunted place in the building. Inside, hair products sometimes flew off the shelves. They didn't just fall off and drop to the floor as they might if the shelves were tilted (which they weren't). The bottles would actually sail through the air.

When they recently streamed music from Pandora in that

room, it sounded like the song was skipping—which shouldn't happen with online music. When they carefully listened to what it was repeating over and over, they heard "Save me! Save me! Save me!"

Two of them got so freaked out, they had to go outside and smoke a cigarette.

She said she had overheard a conversation between two of their bosses discussing good spirits on one side of a door in the building and bad spirits on the other; she was convinced that door was the one to the studio—and the bad spirits were inside.

Faith said her current apartment was also haunted. She kept hearing loud footsteps "upstairs,", but their apartment was on the top floor; there was nothing above them. She didn't mention it to her boyfriend, but he separately noticed the same thing.

Once, in the middle of the night, she also heard footsteps coming up the stairs to their floor and children giggling. She thought it was odd that someone would let their children run around so late. But when she looked through her peephole, she saw no one—and she could see the whole floor because of where their apartment was located.

Faith 2

When I went back to see Faith weeks later, of course we talked about ghosts—but this time not about those at the Masonic Temple.

I was going "up north" for a weekend to an inn that was supposedly haunted (the very one where Vanessa and her husband had seen the shadow walker, although we were not so lucky during our stay). Faith said that when she was a kid, her family had stayed at a waterfront hotel in an old brick building in that town.

She and her brother had decided to go swimming in the pool. As she stood on the edge, she felt hands on her back shoving her into the water. She looked around, but there was no one there. Her brother had the same experience.

They were spooked and went to the front desk to tell them what had happened. The desk clerk admitted that other people had experienced the same thing. They pressed for an explanation, and he said a young girl, around four years old, had drowned in the pool.

She may have been pushed in by her brother. Or was she shoved in by the same entity that was now trying to push in other children? Disturbing in any case—but especially if the ghost was still targeting kids!

Faith 3

Once again we discussed the building's haunted basement. Faith said some stylists had decided to use a homemade Ouija board in its most paranormally active studio. She left the room because she wanted no part of it.

We discussed how dangerous Ouija boards can be, because you can't control who or what comes through, and nasty spirits can become attached to you. She said the same women used their Ouija board at one of their friend's houses, and her coworker's whole personality changed. "She seemed to go crazy."

Faith genuinely wondered if she had become possessed.

Julie

Just a couple of weeks before everything shut down due to COVID, a new stylist showed me her Ouija planchette tattoo, depicting the triangular piece that moves around the board to point to letters. Despite her tat, she agreed that she would never use a Ouija board because of the dangers.

She said when she was a child, she used to visit her uncle, who lived in the oldest house in the county—it had been built around an ancient log cabin. Upstairs, three bedrooms had been turned into a loft. She would go up there to read—and several times she saw a lady all in white, which scared her.

Her uncle kept decorative mugs on a high shelf in the kitchen with the handles facing outward, so he could grab them easily. When he came down in the morning, all of the handles would be pointed inward. No one could reach the shelf but him. He would change the direction of all the handles, but it would happen again.

BEYOND POLTERGEISTS

"Keep some room in your heart for the unimaginable."
—Mary Oliver

After I learned that ghosts were real, I wanted to find out as much as I could about them—and hopefully encounter more. Whenever my husband and I went on vacation, I would seek to stay in a haunted B & B or hotel.

I dragged poor David on numerous "ghost tours" in historic towns and cities. Although these tours were primarily designed for entertainment, some genuinely offered ghostly evidence.

I'm happy to say, as the years have passed, I've had more paranormal experiences beyond that first poltergeist.

Historic Haunts

David and I had arranged to vacation in Philadelphia during the Fourth of July week—spurred by our desire to visit our daughter during her internship at Longwood Gardens. I love history, ancient places and ghosts—so of course I signed us up for a ghost tour one evening. It was one of the highlights of our trip—especially because it made us realize we may already have encountered some of the city's ghosts without even realizing it.

**

On the Sunday before the ghost tour, we visited the well-preserved 18th century Bishop White House. Our small group (my husband, daughter, me, and just one other man) was led to the house by a ranger from the Park Service, which oversaw the site. He unlocked the door and quickly went into his spiel.

Suddenly we heard loud knocking. The Ranger said "Oh, that's probably just someone who wants to join our tour. Let's ignore it." Something seemed a bit "off" about it; he seemed unnerved. I thought, what's with this guy?

Then a loud alarm went off. The Ranger seemed a bit flustered, but said, "That's the motion detector; it's over-sensitive." He tried to turn off the alarm but couldn't. Again, he said, "We'll just ignore it," as he continued leading us upstairs on our tour.

I thought it was a cool old house with an amazing history but didn't connect the dots until the young guide for our ghost tour took us back to the Bishop White House at the beginning of our evening tour.

She said the house was so haunted, the Park Service couldn't get any of their employees to stay there as caretakers—although they usually had on-site caretakers at historic properties.

Our ghost tour guide told us of tragic deaths in the house: Bishop White's mother and sister from yellow fever, later his wife and daughter from dysentery—most likely because they had put their latrine in the house, right next to the kitchen—a "modern convenience" that contaminated their food.

She said odd things were always happening in the house: doors opening and closing, lights going off and on, etc.—and that sometimes the apparition of a woman could be seen in the kitchen window.

Our guide urged us to take photographs of the kitchen in the twilight. We were standing in the garden next to the house property; normally the ghost tour couldn't get that close, but the garden happened to be open that night.

One man in our group took a photo he immediately showed us all: it looked like the shape of a woman's head and shoulders all in white, silhouetted in the window. You couldn't see fine details, but the shape was pretty amazing. We could not see it with our eyes when looking at the window. But the camera had caught it. It reminded me of EVPS, with their ghost voices caught by digital recorders that our ears don't hear.

As we were walking between sites, I sidled up next to our guide and asked if she had personally had any paranormal experiences. She said yes, they used to take ghost tours to the Pine Street Church and Graveyard. But they stopped because so many things happened there. Cell phone and camera batteries that had just been charged would suddenly go dead and kids, who are often more sensitive to ghosts, would get very upset. The tour company became increasingly afraid that someone would get hurt and eventually decided it was safer to cut that haunted location from the tour.

Her explanation was chilling, because the day before, when David and I had wandered around photographing the oldest churches and graveyards in the city (I love old buildings and gravestones.) I had gone up the steps in front of the Pine Street Church. I took a single photo and my camera battery suddenly went completely dead without warning (it usually warned me if the battery was getting low) and the camera shut down.

I had been upset at the time because I had planned to take a lot more photos as we walked back through Society Hill in the twilight. I couldn't understand why my battery had gone dead.

Now I realized a ghost may have destroyed my plans to capture those photographs.

* * *

Galena Ghosts

At the end of a ghost tour we took in Galena, Illinois, the guide asked if any of us had ever had any ghostly encounters. No one spoke up at first, so I broke the ice and told them about my initial experience with the poltergeist.

Then a man and his wife talked about their experiences. Although their house was not very old—it was built in 1960— the man had seen a ghostly woman walk down the stairs in a white robe on several occasions.

He had also heard the sound of the door opening and shutting, and footsteps crossing the floor. Thinking it was his wife back from grocery shopping, he went to help her with the groceries, only to find that no one was there. A sister-in-law who was staying with them had the same thing happen to her, and she was so freaked out that she now refuses to stay in the house alone.

After the tour group had dispersed, we continued our conversation. The man said that before the haunting had happened in their house, he had "never believed in ghosts or any of that stuff."

Then they had decided to visit the graveyard where famous "Indian Lydia" was buried (she died in 1866 in Illinois). It had become known for paranormal activity. The man said that in the graveyard. he had seen little white and red glowing orbs. Most of his friends and his wife couldn't see the glowing orbs, so he told them where to aim their cameras to take photographs of them. Fortunately, the orbs showed up in their pictures.

Only one of his friends could see the orbs as he did. She held out her hands but as one of the orbs got close to her, she could no longer see it. She said," It's above my hands now, isn't it? I can feel the heat." He could still see it and confirmed that she was correct.

The man said that his wife doesn't see most of the paranormal things that he does. I suggested he may be psychic. He said he thought that everyone was, in some way. I agreed.

After he left the hotel lobby, one of the women from the tour walked up to me. She wanted to tell me about her experiences, although she hadn't told the whole group when she'd had the opportunity. She said lots of things had happened when she was growing up in her "mother's house."

One day, she ran upstairs to her bedroom to find a little girl crying, and a woman sitting on her bed, comforting the girl. They were both ghosts. That freaked her out and she ran back downstairs.

She asked her mother about the apparitions and was told that they were the ghosts of her grandmother and one of her children who had been bitten by a dog. It sounded like several generations of the family had lived in that same house.

I asked if she had seen the little girl again and she said yes, with the woman. She said her mother has had all kinds of paranormal experiences in the house, but it doesn't freak them out too much now, since the ghosts don't seem to mean any harm. And, after all, they are the relatives of those living there.

At breakfast at our B&B the next morning, my husband and I talked about the ghost tour and I asked the proprietor if she had ever experienced anything paranormal. She hesitated, but then admitted that they had. Not in the guesthouse where we were staying, but in their house. (I wondered if the guest house might be haunted too, but she didn't want that getting out).

She said that a model at a figure drawing class had seen a woman in a long dress staring at her from one of the windows in their house. Her husband had also heard footsteps when no one was there.

She also mentioned that in the early 1930s their house had been a restaurant. It had just closed for the night when there was a knock on the door. The family's teenage daughter/waitress answered and a very nice man politely said he knew that they were closed, but was there any chance that he and his friends could get a meal? They had just arrived from Chicago and couldn't find a place to eat, and he and his friends were hungry.

The family agreed to feed them, and the visitors had a nice dinner there. They asked for someone to guard their car while they ate, and one of the family's sons did so. The man left a stunning $50 tip for the family.

Later, they saw the man's photograph in a newspaper and recognized him. The man they had fed was John Dillinger. When they asked their son, who had guarded the car, if he had seen anything unusual, he said he just saw lots of little black suitcases sitting in the car.

Many years later, when the teenage girl/waitress was an elderly lady in a nursing home, she was eager to tell everyone of her encounter with the famous gangster, who had been very nice to them.

We wondered if that event had led her to remain in the house as a ghost.

The proprietor of the guest house told us that lots of places in Galena are purportedly haunted, but many hotel and restaurant owners didn't want word to get out because it might scare off customers.

However, she had heard that the people renovating an old building on Main Street into the One Eleven restaurant had experienced all kinds of paranormal activity. In fact, she said the family had been intending to live on the third floor of the building, but the wife refused to move there because of all the ghostly activity—which seemed most intense on the third floor.

Of course, we headed to One Eleven Main for dinner. The charming restaurant was on the first floor of a brick building, with big windows facing Main Street. I had a very delicious BBQ pork sandwich. After dinner, I asked our waiter if he had ever experienced any paranormal activity there and he replied with a resounding "Yes!" He said he had photos. If we were willing to wait, he'd get them.

He showed us three large photos that he said had been taken with a good 35mm camera (not digital) on the third floor. The first photo showed a red glowing "scribbly" line that moved around chaotically. There was also a glowing white line that looked as if a glowing dot had been caught moving rapidly through the air.

They reminded me of the man from the ghost tour who said he had seen both red and white glowing orbs zooming around a cemetery. This is how I expected those orbs would look if caught by a camera in flight.

There was also a misty-looking white shape in the middle of the first photo that looked like a head forming. In the second photo, that shape had grown into what looked like a human figure. In the third photo, a white/misty woman appeared to be flying across the frame. You could see her face and bust, with her arms out in front, her dress and hair flying backward as she flew to the right.

It was amazing! He said he had shown the pictures to experts and they believe that they're real—they didn't see how he could have faked them with his camera and film.

The server invited us to go up to the third floor to take some photos ourselves. He had sent another group up and they had apparently gotten some great photos which they had promised to email to him.

I was excited to go up to the third floor and I took lots of photos of the empty space there, with beautiful huge old windows looking down on Main Street. But unfortunately, my digital photos did not show anything unusual.

After we checked into our second B&B, we went up into our room's tower to relax in the whirlpool tub, with its electric wall fireplace and twinkling lights setting a lovely mood. My husband decided to go downstairs to shave and brush his teeth. I heard him yell something up at me. He called up a second time. It may have been, "Honey!" It wasn't completely clear, but I heard a "nee" at the end.

When he didn't say anything more, I wondered what he wanted. I finally called "David!" a couple of times. When he came up the stairs, I asked what he had wanted. He was confused. I told him I had heard him calling, but he said he hadn't said anything, he had just heard me call for him.

He hadn't heard the voice that I had heard, but he said his electric toothbrush might have drowned it out. He suggested that I might have heard someone in the room next door. However, there was no one sleeping in the room next to ours. There were people two rooms distant, but since it was midnight, would someone have been yelling loud enough at that hour to be heard all the way to our room? My gut was saying I had just heard something paranormal. But I couldn't prove it.

I decided to download the photos from our trip onto my laptop so I could look at them in a larger format. But after I'd finished downloading them, only the photos I had taken BEFORE we arrived in Galena showed up.

I was worried that something might have happened to erase all the Galena photos from my camera. But when I looked on the camera, fortunately the Galena photos were still there. Since all of the trip photos from before we reached town had downloaded fine, it didn't seem to be a malfunctioning connector cable.

I tried again to download the Galena photos. But I never could get them to download to the laptop while in that location. I told my husband that it was almost as if a Galena ghost didn't want us to have those pictures!

When we got home, I easily downloaded all of the photos to our PC—including the Galena shots—without a hitch.

It made me wonder if we had inadvertently brought a temporary ghost "guest" from haunted One Eleven Main's third floor to the B&B, and they had been messing with us. Earthbound spirits can get entertainment—and energy—from incidents like this!

Old City Jail

While visiting historic Charleston, South Carolina, David and I took part in a paranormal investigation at the Old City Jail on Magazine Street. The building is reputed to be the most haunted place in the state. Many people died there—and a woman who supposedly murdered numerous people was held there before she was publicly hanged.

Six of us joined the local leader, Janis. She gave us a tour of the three floors still remaining from when the jail was originally built in 1802. (The fourth floor was destroyed in an 1886 earthquake and part of the building is so unstable, it's too dangerous to go there.) Among other inmates, pirates had been jailed there in the early 1800's, and later, soldiers from both sides of the Civil War.

On the first floor, reportedly the most paranormally active, people were whipped to death, put in solitary confinement boxes—which look like a coffin with just a narrow slit to breathe through—and a sadistic doctor experimented on people, deliberately torturing them. The kitchen and infirmary were also on that floor.

Up on the second floor, there was a room with a red light and odd shapes and shadows on the walls; we took photos there, hoping to capture something. Across the hall was a room with replicas of the barred cages where people were kept—including Lavinia, supposedly the first female serial killer in America.

According to the story, she and her husband ran an inn and would poison solitary travelers so they could rob them and bury them under the building. They supposedly did this for a whole year until one target didn't drink the drugged tea and then lie down on his bed, which normally dropped unconscious victims down a trap door to where Lavinia and her husband stabbed them to death. The one man who escaped death alerted authorities.

Some think that Lavinia and her husband may have robbed people but not necessarily murdered them. However, Lavinia, who was very beautiful, was packed into a tiny cell with a dozen murderers and rapists who probably abused her horribly while she awaited her hanging. Horrifying things happened to people in that place.

The quarters of the warden, his wife, and their children, were next to the cells where they kept the murderers and rapists. I can't imagine living there or raising children in that environment.

One room had a large, odd-looking door that was added later and is supposedly a portal, perhaps because a Ouija board was used in that area.

There was an antique wooden wheelchair on the third floor that I found both creepy and fascinating. Reportedly, the ghost of the youngest prisoner, a ten-year-old black boy, has been known to make the wheelchair move across the floor. That poor child had been sent to the prison for accidentally causing the death of a man when he released the brake on a streetcar. He probably died there.

After our introduction to the jail, David and I wandered around, armed with EMF meters, a Ghost Box, (which scans AM radio frequencies to create white noise and detect EVPs), and a screw-on flashlight. Unfortunately, no ghosts turned on my flashlight—and the Ghost Box was too garbled to understand.

I took a lot of photos, both with and without flash, in the various rooms. Right after I took a shot of the ancient wheelchair, I realized I had captured what appeared to be a vivid streak of light slipping through the chair's back slats. When I showed it to Janis, she asked me to send the photo to her.

At one point, Janis used dousing rods to talk to "Animal" who she said was a "simple" young man who used to crawl on all fours; she said he was friendly and liked to flirt with pretty girls. She didn't think he was there when the building was a prison but when it was an asylum.

After that, we all went outside with our EMF meters to try to identify where the gallows had been. At one spot, all our EMF meters went crazy—lighting up to the highest level—suggesting that was where the hangings had occurred.

I felt a bit ill the whole time I was inside the jail, but thought it was just due to the late hour (we were there from about midnight until 3 am) or maybe my stomach was irritated from hunger. However, as soon as we stepped outside, I felt much better.

One of the investigators told me that feeling ill at a haunted location may be a sign that you're sensitive—and if ghosts make signs around you, it may be that they recognize your abilities before you do. (That was in response to me telling them about my original poltergeist experience and the knocking we heard in Philadelphia.)

Ontonagon, Michigan

While we were driving around Lake Superior on vacation, a flying rock apparently put a big hole in our transmission. We had to be towed to the nearest town—20 miles away—which turned out to be charming Ontonagon, Michigan. We were stuck there for days while the only auto repair shop in town tried to obtain the part needed to fix our car.

Surprisingly, it turned out to be one of our most fun and memorable trips (despite the large repair bill). Among other adventures, we rappelled down mine shafts in an old, abandoned copper mine (I volunteered to go first) and toured the Ontonagon lighthouse courtesy of the local historical society.

We learned that structure was built in 1866 and heard stories about the lighthouse keepers and their wives, including one who had died in her thirties after having eight kids. Another wife only had two sons survive out of her four children. Times were hard in the nineteenth century.

Of course, I asked about ghosts. The tour guides said the building's doors would regularly open and close by themselves.

While in the lighthouse alone, a docent decided to sweep the floors, and temporarily put rugs on chairs to get them out of the way. When she returned from sweeping another room, she found the rugs back on the floor. No one else was present.

Rumpled rugs would also often get straightened out by unseen hands. Apparently, the ghosts wanted things "just so."

One day, a docent heard metal clinking on the long stairs that led up to the top of the lighthouse. They went to investigate and found an ancient oil can—the oldest artifact in the whole place—sitting on a step by itself halfway up the stairs. No one else was there at the time.

A longtime volunteer had a great-granddaughter who saw a pillow she owned that was embroidered with the lighthouse. The girl said she wanted to go see the little blonde girl in the lighthouse window named Alice. When the woman brought her great-granddaughter to the lighthouse, she immediately started talking to an invisible ghost girl that nobody else could see and spent her whole time there chatting with her. Later, the woman learned that a little blonde girl had died at the lighthouse—and her name was Alice.

Palmer House, Sauk Centre

We had an opportunity to go back to the haunted Palmer House for a supernatural event with Dave Schrader and Shane Pittman of "The Holzer Files" and other TV ghost shows, Sarah Lemos, psychic medium on various television programs, and Bill Chappell, engineering wizard of the ghost hunting world.

We each assembled a Ghost Box under Chappell's tutelage and I was able to put mine to good use that very night, when we roamed the hotel from the basement to the third floor, seeking to engage the resident spirits.

We got some decent EVPs and answers on the Ghost Box with small groups of other investigators.

But eventually just my husband and I settled into the children's playroom on the third floor. I revved up my newly minted Ghost Box and started asking the ghost kids questions. David recorded everything on his phone, which was super helpful. It allowed me to go back and listen to the session, so I could catch and confirm words I might have missed in the moment.

"What's your name?" I asked.

"Mike."

"Do you want me to read to you?

"Yes."

I walked over to a rack holding board books and chose one with a barn on the front.

"Do you want this book?

"Yeah!" It certainly *did* sound like a kid's voice.

I started reading and asking the young ghosts questions.

"Counting on the Farm. Wake up, wake up, the sun is out. From one to ten, it's fun to count. Can you count?"

"Yeah."

"Colors in the Barnyard. How many colors can you see?" No response.

"Do you see red?"

"Red!" came very clearly from the Ghost Box.

"Good job!" I said.

Another page showed different shapes found on the farm. "Look at all the shapes. Do you see anything round in this picture?" I asked.

"Yolk."

"There are apples..." I said.

"Egg!"

"...Pumpkins, fruit." I continued.

"Fruit!" Then, "Pump." There *was* a handpump in the picture.

Another page showed kids doing chores around the farm. "Chore time. Do you like doing chores?" I asked.

"Yeah."

"Or would you rather play? It looks like they're hard at work!"

"Yeah."

The final pages showed a bunch of animals making noises. "And then we have the animal sounds. Who makes the quack, quack noise?" I asked.

"Frog!"

That really confused me. I thought that I had misheard the kids—or that they were teasing me. Later, I played the recording back repeatedly trying to figure the word out, but it sure sounded like "frog." Then I searched online for quacking noises and frogs. Up popped articles on how a wood frog chorus sounds like quacking ducks! The males start "quacking" around early April, which was close to the time I was visiting with the children. Maybe living out in the country—probably during an earlier time, before TV, video games and phones took over kids' lives—had made the ghost children more aware of the sounds of animals in nature. I could certainly imagine that catching frogs might have been one of their pastimes.

"What animal says woof, woof?" No response.

"What animal says baa, baa?"

"Lamb."

"What animal says oink, oink, oink?" No response.

"What's your favorite animal?"

"Lamb." There was a pause and then, "Pig!" (Maybe two different kids weighed in.)

"I have a cat. Do you like cats?" No response.

"Do you like cats or dogs better?"

"Dogs!" There was a pause. "Both!"

"You like both? I kind of like both too." I wondered if they had just added "both" to be nice to me since I had said I had a cat. Or again, perhaps two different kids had expressed their opinions.

"I also have pet snakes. Do you like snakes?"

There was a loud but unclear response.

"What do you think of snakes?" I asked. They answered with a whole sentence that I couldn't decipher. (It may not have been complimentary.)

"Would you like to see a snake?"

"Snake!" They said as I was asking the question.

"Do you want me to read you another book?"

"Yes!"

However, I couldn't read to the kids again as we were called downstairs. It was late and our time to investigate the hotel was over. But I was thrilled with how responsive the ghost children had been. I wished I could give them each a hug.

HOME SWEET HAUNTED HOME

"Certain old houses demand to be haunted..."
—Robert Louis Stevenson

Although I've had paranormal experiences on the road, I no longer feel the need to seek out haunted locations during vacations to encounter ghosts. One Halloween I bought a cute little sign that says it all—and stays up all year: "Home Sweet Haunted Home."

Lights On

David was awakened late one night by the hall light coming on. It's at the top of the staircase landing on the second story that leads to the hallway connecting three upstairs bedrooms and a bathroom in our 1920s home. David thought our son had returned home and thoughtlessly turned on the light, which shone brightly into the open doorway of our bedroom. He waited for our son to turn it off.

When the light still wasn't turned off after quite a while, David got up, annoyed, intending to ask our son to shut off the light. He then discovered that our son was NOT home yet. He turned off the hallway light and went back to bed.

About ten minutes later, the light came on again. Once more, David got up and turned it off. I slept through it all (darn it); my only excuse being I am further from the door and face the wall away from it.

When David told me about it the next morning, he teased me, saying "I blame you!" claiming I brought a ghost home with one of my many antiques. In reality, he wasn't sure he believed in ghosts and thought it might be due to old wiring or a faulty light switch.

Lights On 2

In the dining room one evening, right before bed, I turned off seasonal decorative lights that were hanging over the buffet. I pivoted to the dining room table to grab a book I intended to bring upstairs. When I turned around, the decorative lights were back on. This happened shortly after the episode in the hallway upstairs.

Bone Dice

On All Saints Day one year, I decided to use the new pair of bone dice I had just bought from Viking reenactors at "Loki's party" at the American Swedish Institute.

I said aloud that these were my new bone dice and if any ghosts or spirits were present, I asked them to please make the dice roll two sixes.

After I shook up the dice quite thoroughly and dropped them onto the counter, a bit of a shock went through me because I really didn't expect to get two sixes. There they were.

I wondered if it actually meant there was a cooperative ghost around—or if I had just shaken a lucky 1-in-36 double-sixes. (There's a 2.77 percent chance of rolling a pair of sixes—*without* the help of ghosts.)

I rolled the dice many more times to see if the handcrafted cubes tended to roll sixes more often than other numbers, but I didn't see two sixes again.

I did not demand further proofs from any attending spirits at that time because I wasn't sure it was a good idea to encourage them to engage in more activity inside our house.

Every time something happens in our house that could possibly be paranormal, I don't assume it actually is. Maybe I just happened to get a "lucky" shake. Maybe our old house has iffy wiring and lights come on by themselves.

But some things are harder to explain away.

Cat Got Your Ghost

In late 2017, we lost our two beloved cats that we had adopted from the local Humane Society as kittens in 1999. Sweet, amiable Nightshade went downhill abruptly and passed quite unexpectedly in mid-September. Then, petite little Cuzzy (just 4 pounds), a gorgeous and devoted tortoiseshell, left us in early December. She had stopped eating and using her litter box and was in the last stages of kidney failure.

I held her tenderly and told her I loved her as the vet who came to our home gave her the injection that put her out of her misery. Then I sobbed so hard. My heart was broken.

A week or two after Cuzzy died, I was sitting at the computer in our family room and felt a cat rub against my leg. I looked down, shocked, but saw nothing. It sure felt like a cat, but we no longer had any cats. I thought I must be imagining things and said nothing to anyone.

A week later, my husband said, "I don't know if I should mention this, but I swear I felt a cat rub against my leg. I leaned over to pet it, forgetting we no longer had any cats, and of course, there was nothing there."

I stared at him. "Where were you sitting when this happened?"

"At the computer in the family room."

Exactly where I had experienced the same thing.

I was so grateful that David had mentioned his experience because it validated mine. I no longer doubted that Cuzzy had come for a visit in ghost form. While alive, she had often sought our attention in the same way when we spent more time interacting with the internet than with her. It was only appropriate that she would reach out to us one last time in that same place.

Neither of us ever received another visit from Cuzzy. I believe that she had come one last time to each of us to say goodbye and then had gone into the light—to the better place where she belonged. It was a gift that soothed my hurting heart.

Victorian Push Sleigh

In early November 2019, I bought a Victorian child's push sleigh that I saw for sale in an online marketplace; it was located in a nearby town. I drove over to the seller's house to see the sleigh after an earlier "buyer" who claimed that she wanted it never showed up.

The woman who sold it to me said that her parents had bought the sleigh in the 1950s from an antiques dealer around the time that she had been born and it had been in her family ever since. She was happy to see it go to a good home where someone would cherish it.

I collect antique dolls (yes, I know, many people think they look creepy—probably due to Hollywood horror movies) and I thought they would look adorable in the sleigh with a blanket tucked around them.

As soon as I paid the seller, she went back inside her house. I carefully placed the sleigh on the flattened passenger seat of my car.

Right after I slid into the driver's seat, something hit me hard on the forehead and bounced off. I looked up, trying to figure out what could have hit me and saw that my garage door opener was missing from its holder on the visor of the car. The holder keeps the opener quite secure; it had never fallen off before.

In fact, if it had somehow gotten loose, I would have expected it to just fall to the car floor—not fly horizontally at me. I found the little rectangular opener and snapped it back into the holder.

At that point, I wondered if there was a cranky ghost attached to the antique sleigh—maybe a little boy or girl who had once loved it. Or the parents of the woman who had sold it to me, who wished she had kept it in the family? I decided I'd better lay down some ground rules, just in case.

I said, "If there's someone attached to this sleigh, that's okay. I have no problems with ghosts—they're just people without bodies. But NO harming anyone in my house or harassing my cat. Everyone needs to get along." Nothing else happened on the way home to suggest a disgruntled ghost was coming along with the sleigh. Hopefully, the flying garage door opener had been a fluke.

My husband had been out of town at a writers' convention when I bought the sleigh and knew nothing about it. I put it in an empty upstairs bedroom, planning to bring it down and put it in front of our fireplace for Christmas.

When David returned home, he complained that his coffee maker was suddenly acting weird. When he poured water in, it only gave him half a cup of coffee, instead of a full cup. It had never done that before. Hmmmm, I thought.

At work, my computer phone started randomly calling people through Skype. The company's IT expert had no idea why that was happening or how to stop it. It had never done that before. I wondered if a ghost attached to the sleigh could have followed me to work.

A week later, I heard a very loud knock downstairs in the middle of the night and one morning shortly after that I heard another one (David was asleep). Hmmmm, again.

On December 1st (our wedding anniversary), I woke early (as usual) and decided to listen to a favorite CD. The portable CD player kept playing the first song over and over, no matter what buttons I pushed. The song I couldn't get it to move off of was "Counting Stars" by One Republic, with lyrics including "Lately I've been, I've been losing sleep..." (true—very funny), "Everything that kills me makes me feel alive..." Well, if a ghost wanted to send me a message, they could do worse than picking that song.

Hot Tempered

I have some reptiles that require tropical temperatures, and a thermostat keeps the heat within safe parameters in their enclosures. I noticed that the temperature was suddenly way up in some of the tanks and it needed to be kept in the 80s. Three times the temperature spiked dangerously high, and three times, I turned it back down. I was upset. The temperatures had never changed on their own before.

I finally decided if a ghost was at fault, I needed to lay down the law. I spoke aloud and firmly said if anyone was changing the temperatures, they needed to stop it! "You may just be playing around—but those high temperatures could harm or even kill the animals and they are nice creatures that never did anyone any harm. I will NOT put up with that! I will NOT allow you to harm my animals! I will banish you if you continue doing that!"

It never happened again.

Meandering Stones

While at a meeting of the Minnesota Herpetological Society (herpetology is the zoology of reptiles and amphibians), I felt coolness on the back of my thigh, as if water were running down my leg. I felt the back of my leggings, wondering how they could have gotten wet.

I didn't feel any moisture. But there was a lump inside the cloth. I slowly pushed it down to the ankle opening and was surprised to see a small green flat stone pop out—aventurine—that I had bought a few weeks earlier.

I had no idea how it could have gotten into my leggings at that moment. I had driven to the meeting and had not felt or noticed anything unusual. There were no pockets in my clothing that it could have fallen from and somehow slipped into my tight leggings.

A couple of days later, David brought me a small amethyst stone and said he had found it in the laundry room and wondered how it had gotten there. I didn't know.

The last time I had seen the stone, it had been on our bed where I had found it while sorting through some things. Had our cat somehow batted the rock off the bed, over the rugs, into the closet, and down the clothes chute? It seemed unlikely, but who knows?

Cat Jump

Early one morning, while I was with our cat Lily in the dining room, I heard what sounded like a cat jumping down onto the kitchen floor. I went into the adjoining kitchen and looked all over but couldn't find anything that might have fallen and made a sound. Was it a return visit by Cuzzy or Nightshade?

Agate Dice

In early 2020, I bought an agate cube and thought it would make a lovely die. So I found little colored stickers, cut them in circles and put one color on each side of the cube: purple, pink, blue, green, orange, and yellow. The sides of the cube weren't perfectly even. Yellow and green were the largest sides and pink was the smallest.

I decided to try the new die out right after I made it. I remembered my experience with the bone dice and thought, what the heck, why not see if I get a response with this die made of natural material too?

I said aloud, "if there are any ghosts here, please make the purple side come up." I rolled and bounced the die and the purple side came up on top. I said, "Well that's interesting."

As I had with the bone dice, I rolled the stone cube repeatedly to see if it just tended to naturally roll purple. It did not. It rolled all the different colors with less likelihood for purple than some of the other colors.

Months later, I decided to try rolling the agate cube with the colored spots again. First, I said, "If there are any ghosts or spirits here, please make the green spot come up on top." Sure enough, it did.

Generally, with a cube, there would be a 1 in 6 chance of rolling any particular color. Not unbelievable odds by any means—but it was still interesting that the only two times I had asked ghosts/spirits to give me a specific result when rolling the die, I got the outcome I requested. (I would expect that if there were NO ghosts present, I would not get the requested results.)

Surprise Opening

I inherited an old wooden case with a printed image of the face of Jesus in a frame on the front, and items stored inside that a priest could use for administering the Last Rites if a person were dying. A latch on top held the picture frame lid tightly to the wooden case behind it.

One morning the framed lid suddenly popped open and things flew out of the case, surprising me and the cat. I found a candle, a spoon and two tiny crystal bowls (probably for oil and holy water) that had fallen out.

The latch was so tight that I had to use pliers to get it back into its loop—so clearly the latch couldn't easily have come undone by itself.

Tip from a Ghost

In April of 2020, I came downstairs in the morning to find that a small wooden stool, normally situated in front of my 1760s Queen Anne side chair, had been flipped upside down and was a couple of feet away from where it normally stood. The antique photo album and Victorian ceramic tray that normally sat on the stool were on the floor right in front of the chair. Fortunately, the tray wasn't broken.

Could our cat Lily have squeezed behind the chair and run into the stool, knocking it over? I had never seen her back there before (or since) and she didn't normally knock anything over.

Of course, the chair and stool sat right next to the Victorian push sleigh. Perhaps the ghost that may have come with it was trying to let us know they were still around?

Garage Ghost

My son, daughter, and her fiancé, joined us in our huge, detached garage in late October, with the wood stove stoked, to celebrate my daughter's birthday in a safe, socially distant manner. After dinner, she started opening gifts.

Since Halloween was just three days away, instead of putting a bow on her present, I had made a tassel out of fuzzy white yarn and inked in black eyes so that it looked like a ghost.

"It's so cute! I love your ghost!" said my daughter.

At that exact moment, several things fell off the back wall of the garage onto the work bench below with a loud clatter. I started laughing. Apparently one of our ghosts had joined the party and wanted to let us know that he appreciated my daughter's comment.

My daughter didn't think it was so funny; she said real ghosts creeped her out.

Alexa Answers

We have Alexa, the interactive, talking speaker with a Wi-Fi connection. When you say "Alexa" a ring around the cylinder lights up in blue, and she responds to your question or command.

I've come to suspect that ghosts and spirits may be able to manipulate Alexa just as they can with digital recordings and other electronics.

One evening, I was sitting in my living room and I spoke aloud to all of my grandparents (who have passed) because I know they can hear me on the other side. I said "Thank you so much for all that you did for me and all the love you gave me. I love you so much and I know I will see you again. THANK YOU!"

Alexa then responded, "You're welcome." I had NOT mentioned her name to activate her, so that made me laugh. I felt that my grandparents had sent me a message through Alexa. She has never responded since then with "you're welcome" when I said "thank you" without my first saying her name to activate her.

Another day, I was brushing my cat, Lily, and thought it might be fun to stroke in rhythm to a cat song. I said, "Alexa, play "Three little kittens have lost their mittens"; I didn't know the exact title so I gave that first lyric of the song.

Suddenly a woman began talking about communicating with our loved ones who had died. What?! I hadn't known that Alexa could play audible books—and I certainly hadn't requested that topic. How did "three little kittens" bring me "talking to the dead"? Again, I felt a spirit or ghost who was present may have manipulated Alexa to give me a sign—a way of saying "Hi, I'm here."

Holiday Shenanigans

In December of 2021, our Christmas tree lights (the same ones we had used for years) started turning themselves off—and then, a little while later. turning back on. The action would often repeat at random intervals. This happened on quite a few occasions.

While I was working on this book on our computer in the family room, the television behind me suddenly turned on. I thought my husband might have used the remote, but he wasn't anywhere to be seen. I found him and asked if he had turned on the TV and he didn't know what I was talking about.

This reminded me of the previous month, when my mother, siblings, and their spouses joined David and me at our family cabin. It was November and we were doing some hard work when we decided to take the opportunity to share an early Thanksgiving dinner together. A lamp in the living room kept going off and then turning back on.

My brother thought something was wrong with the bulb and changed it. The lamp continued to go off and on. He couldn't figure it out. But some of us had a pretty good idea of who might be doing it—the beloved relative you'll read about next.

EARTHBOUND SPIRITS GET PERSONAL

"Wonder is the beginning of wisdom."
—*Socrates*

On May 15, 2016, my mother, and all of us children (and some grandchildren), were with my Dad as he quietly passed away. He was 90 and had been declining, so it wasn't a shock. But I had never lost anyone so close to me before.

I wept as I wrote his eulogy; I was afraid I would break into tears as I delivered it at his funeral, but somehow, I made it through. I felt that he was there—and I hoped that he liked what I had said.

In the fall, my husband and I traveled to New Orleans for the first time, and I decided to visit a psychic medium, which I had never done before. New Orleans has a reputation for paranormal activity and spiritual practitioners, so it seemed like a fun thing to do while on vacation.

I spent an hour with the guy I had chosen, based on positive online reviews I had seen before we arrived in town. He said some interesting things that could have indicated my Dad was with us—but nothing definitive. It was fun but I wasn't convinced mediums actually spoke with the dead.

The most encouraging thing he said was that Dad was trying to communicate with me; he suggested that I take a bath (since I was a water sign, a Cancer like him), light a candle, and be open to it.

When a well-known TV medium came to town, I went to her large event with thousands of people. She said things like, "Has someone over here lost a grandma?" (Who hadn't in that crowd?) She suggested that a grieving family had brought something with them that had belonged to their loved one (many do) and they seemed thrilled that she "knew" that.

I thought she seemed much more precise and accurate on TV—and wondered if the crowd was just too big and over-whelming for her to get specific details.

Later I went to a smaller gathering with another TV psychic when he was in town, and I was blown away by the specific details and names he got when bringing forth my father. I was thrilled my Dad was one of the few who came through.

However, before the event, we were required to give the names of everyone in our group who would be attending, which I thought was a little concerning. That would give him the means to look up details about everyone on social media beforehand.

Then the New York Times ran an expose of the man; it sounded like he was getting at least some of his information from social media. I was saddened by that, because it meant that my Dad may not have come through as I had hoped.

But who needs mediums, anyway? Spirits can come through to us more directly.

One night, I dreamt my extended family was at our house for a gathering. I was in the kitchen with my brother and nephew.

Suddenly, my Dad flew/fell across the kitchen from above, landing on the floor of the dining room on his right side. He appeared younger than when he had died, probably in his 60s, and looked well. I knelt down on the floor beside him and started crying and said, "I've missed you so much since you've been gone." He answered firmly, "I'm not gone. I'm right here."

An electric shock went through me. I immediately woke and sensed he was indeed right there beside me.

Loved ones can sometimes reach you in your dreams, when your mind is quieter than during the busy, hectic daytime. When spirits visit from the other side, the dream is more vivid and feels more "real" than normal. I was certain that I had experienced such a "visitation."

Years later, the memory remains vivid.

In 2020, I asked a local psychic who was doing a group Zoom session if she thought ghosts were more active during the pandemic. She said they felt the static from everything that was happening; the energy was higher and there was lots of fear.

She asked if I thought my house was haunted.

I responded by inquiring if she could sense a ghost in my home through Zoom. She said she didn't feel we had a permanent, attached ghost but that we got drive-by ghosts. In fact, she claimed she saw a little girl over my left shoulder. I asked, "She's here now?" and her answer was yes.

I thought that was interesting, because earlier, another local psychic had said that she saw a little ghost girl in my house and when I asked why she was there, the psychic had said that the ghost was attracted to my energy. I was skeptical; surely a ghost girl would be drawn more to my antique dolls and toys than to me! Or had she come with the Victorian push sleigh?

The year 2020 was terrible on so many levels. But it opened up some wonderful opportunities that would not have occurred otherwise. Connecting with a renowned ghost psychic via Zoom was one of them. (She requested that I not reveal her name, since she's trying to retire. She gets a ridiculous number of phone calls, and doesn't want even more. I'll call her Morgan.)

Although I had never watched the TV show Morgan inspired during the five seasons it was on the air, after I had my poltergeist experience, I started devouring books on ghosts. That's when I discovered her book, and learned that from the time she was an infant, she had been able to see ghosts everywhere, all the time.

I tried calling Morgan's phone number a couple of times over the years to see if she could give me any insight into potential ghosts in my house, but she never returned my calls. She later told me that ghosts can prevent such calls from going through, which probably happened in my case.

When I discovered Morgan was going to do Zoom sessions, limited to a small number of people, each able to ask questions about ghosts in their home, I eagerly signed up. (The cost was surprisingly cheap, and she split it with the metaphysical store setting up the calls, so she clearly wasn't in it for the money.)

In May of 2020, while on a Zoom call with Morgan, I had an experience almost as shocking as the poltergeist that first crashed my world. Because of it, I believe she is the real deal.

She explained to everyone on the call that she can only see earthbound spirits (which most people call ghosts). She is not a medium and cannot see or communicate with spirits that have crossed over to the other side.

Morgan also said she had discovered she could see ghosts via Zoom but could not communicate with them telepathically as she normally did when she was in the same location as they were. However, she would be able to let us know if we had any earthbound spirits in our homes and could describe them to us.

When it was my turn, I asked Morgan if she saw or sensed anything in my house. I was sitting at the dining room table with my back to the living room, so she could see most of that room from my laptop. I thought she might see a little girl hanging out by the Victorian push sleigh in the corner.

I was wrong.

Morgan said, "There's an older man standing behind you." She guessed him to be 85 to 90 years old and said he had a fringe of hair. "He seems very comfortable in your house!" She added, "He died on the 15th of the month."

My heart jumped. My Dad had passed on the 15th of the month when he was 90 years old. He had been mostly bald with a fringe of hair around the sides of his head. My husband and I had bought my parents' house when they retired and moved, so of course my Dad would feel comfortable in it—he had lived in the house for over 25 years.

"It sounds like my Dad!"

"Ask him if he knows you."

I turned around and asked the question aloud to someone I couldn't see, my heart thumping.

"He shook his head yes."

I was stunned. My father was still here! Why on earth was he hanging around?

"He's holding up five fingers."

I said "I'm one of five kids."

"He's visiting all of you."

Morgan said she was surprised he stuck around, given his age. Usually when people that old pass, they move on to the other side.

"Could he be visiting my Mom?"

"Is your Mom in a nursing home?"

"No, an apartment."

Morgan looked thoughtful. "That may be it. He probably stuck around for her."

Then Morgan asked if there was a large building on our property, separate from the house.

A skeptic might suggest she had researched departed loved ones of all the people on the call ahead of time on social media—although NONE of the other ghosts she saw in people's houses were relatives or friends. But I had never posted any photos of that building online—and it was not visible on Google Earth, since it was hidden by mature hedges and trees. How the heck did she know about it?

"We have a large, detached garage as well as the house."

She paused as if seeing something. "It wasn't built at the same time as the house, was it?"

"No. It was built later."

"There is another man who comes in and out—and he hangs out in the garage."

"Is it Mr. Schaub?" That was the man who had built our house in the 1920s and had committed suicide in it.

"Your Dad is shaking his head no."

"Is the other guy okay?"

"Your Dad is shaking his head no again. You might want to start smudging to keep him out. Of course, that might also keep your Dad away."

I didn't like the idea of banishing my Dad. "Is the other guy a danger to us?" I asked.

"He's an energy drain." Ghosts are pure energy. They can't eat so they need to take energy from the living. She said if we have headaches, an upset stomach, or other symptoms like that, a ghost could actually be causing them.

Neither David nor I had such symptoms. I said, "I don't like the idea of smudging if it might keep Dad away."

"It's not like he's there 24/7." She paused. "Do you have a 'yes' or 'no' question for your Dad?"

There had been debate between the five of us kids over whether we should keep or sell my parents' beautiful lake house in the woods now that no one was living in it. I wanted to keep the place as a family retreat. "Should we keep the lake home?"

"He shook his head no."

That surprised and disappointed me. My Dad had adored the lake home he built with my mother. He couldn't wait to retire there when he turned 62. He cultivated big vegetable gardens and built several large garages for all of his stuff.

"Why?" I asked. "Because it's too much work—or too expensive to keep up?"

"He's rubbing his fingers together." She demonstrated rubbing her thumb and first two fingers together. "It's about the money."

How clever of my Dad to find a gesture to indicate that! Of course if Dad was visiting everyone, he must know how all of his kids felt about it. He could hear whatever they said, unaware that he was present. Some of them had probably complained about the cost of the upkeep, taxes, and insurance on the property (which we all shared).

"Who's the Grandma with the flower name?"

"Violet! My Dad's Mom. All of her sisters had flower names."

"Why are you not wearing her ring?"

"I don't have a ring from her. I have one from Vina, my other grandma."

"It's a small ring with a garnet set in it. You're supposed to have it."

That was news to me! Suddenly I was dying to see the ring. I had never met sweet Violet because she had died when my father was still in his teens. I would love to have her ring. Later I looked in the bottom drawer of my mother's old red jewelry box, on the off chance that it might be there, but it wasn't.

I asked my Mom if she knew anything about it, but she didn't. I also asked my siblings to keep an eye out for it while we gradually cleaned out many of my parents' possessions from the lake home.

Although Morgan claimed not to be a traditional psychic, she was clearly able to pick up information from the minds of ghosts, even if she was not in the same physical space with them. That became more and more apparent as I jumped on additional Zoom calls with her, learning more about the earthbound spirits who roamed in and out of my home.

I was hoping to ask my Dad some more questions, so I got on another Zoom call with Morgan in June. I was disappointed to learn that my father wasn't around. Morgan said he was probably at my Mom's or with one of my siblings. "He has a lot of places he can go."

Then she said, "Your husband...House. There's a house name."

"My husband's last name is Housewright."

"This must be your father-in-law."

What? He had died many years earlier, in 2004. We had *both* fathers hanging around?

"It has to be his way all the time." She paused. "He's okay. He's okay with what your husband does." She paused again. "He doesn't like what your husband writes. The content."

I told her my husband wrote mystery novels and had won the Edgar Award from the Mystery Writers of America and lots of other awards, but I didn't think his father had ever read a single one of his son's books. He wasn't a reader.

"Did your in-laws get along?"

"Yes, for the most part."

"Is your mother-in-law still around?"

"Yes."

"He'll probably cross when his wife does. He's probably waiting for her like your father is waiting for your mom. He comes and goes, like your Dad."

Morgan added, "It's unusual to have both fathers hanging around! He looks younger than your Dad."

"He died in his 60s. My Dad was 90." I asked a burning question. "Why is he *here*?"

"He's being nosy."

"What does he want?"

"Nothing. Your Dad was communicative. Your husband's Dad isn't. He's just watching."

My husband David asked me to ask Morgan if there was anything his Dad wanted him to know.

"No. He's not very talkative like your Dad was."

"Where is he right now?"

"He's standing in the hallway where the bedroom is."

"Downstairs in the hallway outside the family room (where I was on Zoom) or upstairs?"

"Upstairs."

I was almost as surprised that David's Dad was around as I was when I learned that my Dad was visiting.

After my first mind-boggling Zoom session with Morgan, I sent her a letter with some questions. At the bottom I mentioned that I had called her a couple of times earlier and left a message but had not heard back from her. I included my phone number and asked if she could call me.

She soon called—and the first thing she said was that she had never received any phone calls from me. She confirmed that a ghost could have interfered with that.

"Are there any ghosts in my house today?"

"Two men. One is your Dad again and one is a younger guy, a new one."

"I thought my Dad would have gone "up north" with my Mom and sister."

"Up north? How much further north can you go in Minnesota?"

I laughed and said yes, we border Canada but there are cabins on lakes that people go to "up north."

"Is that the place you talked about selling? He probably did go up for a few days—but then came back. They don't need a car to get around. They're pure energy. They can go wherever they want."

She added. "He has a lot of energy for being as old as he is. I still really think he's waiting for your Mom!"

Morgan had told everyone on the Zoom call that if you dream of someone, "they're where they're supposed to be."

They have gone into the light and are no longer Earthbound. However, I had dreamt of my Dad very vividly. I asked her about that.

"You probably sensed him nearby as you were sleeping and that affected your dream." She would not be able to see him if he had crossed over—so she said he definitely had NOT crossed over.

My daughter had given me a charm in the shape of a golden sun for Christmas from Morgan's shop. The charm was supposed to prevent earthbound spirits from sapping your energy and possibly making you sick. Morgan confirmed that the charm would keep ghosts three to four feet away and I could even wear it in the shower. (I'm fine with sharing my house with ghosts but I don't want them making me feel tired.)

"You have a lot of activity!" she said. "Your house is very active." Morgan wondered if I lived in a high-density area, since we had a lot of different ghosts coming through.

"We live in a suburb, not an apartment or condo. We do have houses on each side, but they're not that close. However, I do have a lot of antiques."

"That could be it. The odd guy may be attached to something."

"Could I use dice to communicate with my Dad—asking him to roll even numbers for yes and odd for no?"

"I tried that with law enforcement, but I found it's not very accurate." They had been looking for a way to communicate with ghosts when Morgan was not around, as I was.

"Maybe ghosts can't always manipulate the dice correctly?" I asked. I really didn't know how hard it was for them to move objects. Some ghosts clearly had figured out how to do it more dramatically than others. Maybe they had been in spirit form longer? Also, I supposed it was possible another ghost nearby could interfere with the dice and throw off the correct answers, just for the fun of it.

"Can I project my thoughts at ghosts to communicate with

them?"

"I don't think they can read our thoughts," she said. Maybe that was a good thing!

"I'm surprised my father-in-law is still around because he died long before my Dad (who died in 2016)."

"Time isn't the same for them as for us. They don't eat or sleep or pay that much attention, because everything is wide open for them, whereas our lives are so scheduled! They may notice bigger shifts—like the change in seasons or Christmas."

In every encounter with Morgan, whether on Zoom or the phone, I learned something new. So I got on another short Zoom call with her every few months after that for a while. To me, it was well worth it.

My sister Von was open and interested in what Morgan had told me, so she decided to join me on the next Zoom call in June. While I called in from my home as usual, she and our Mom participated from the lake home where my parents had lived for decades; they were up there for the weekend.

My Mom and Von asked Morgan if my Dad was there with them.

"Yes, he is."

"Is he waiting for me?" my Mom asked.

Morgan was diplomatic about it. "I wouldn't say he's "waiting" for you so much. He visits you and all the kids—watching over you. He'll stick around until you're ready to go. and you'll go into the light together."

"Is he going other places besides our houses?" Von asked.

"They can go wherever they want! When I die, I plan to go right into the light. But if I did stick around, I wouldn't hang around in someone's house. I'd go to more interesting places. But people are creatures of habit."

"Do ghosts know what's going on in the world?" Von asked.

"Yes, they can tell what's going on. They know when it's

Christmas and what's happening."

"If Dad were to vote, would he vote for Trump?" Von asked.

"Von!" I cried. My Dad had been a lifelong Republican, so I suspected he would answer yes.

"That's a big thumbs-down!" said Morgan. She laughed and said she'd never had anyone ask that kind of question of a ghost before.

Later Von and I wondered if our Dad knew things about Trump that others didn't, since he could go wherever he wanted, unseen. Maybe he had been spying on Trump and didn't like what he had discovered.

I asked Dad questions through Von and Mom, since he was with them. "Could you do something to let us know when you're visiting us, like turn on a light? Could you make a dice go to even or odd numbers to communicate 'yes' or 'no'? How about flipping a coin for 'yes' or 'no'?"

"He's shaking his head no."

I started thinking about EVPs. "If I use a recorder, can you try to speak on it?" Again, Morgan said he seemed to be saying no; it might be too hard for him to do those things.

"Was the dime in my sock from you?" I had found a dime in the toe of a clean sock when I pulled it on.

"He's saying no—but the quarter was from him!"

That blew me away. I had just found a quarter in an "impossible" place and had wondered how in the heck it had gotten there. I had been so surprised and puzzled that I had put the quarter aside to consider it further. No one else knew about it.

"Should I watch for more quarters as a sign from him?"

"He's showing his pockets are empty. He's out of money." Morgan indicated that my Dad was pulling out the linings of his pockets, a clever way to say "no money". I thought that was funny.

"Can our cat Lily see him?"

"Yes." She said that animals will look upwards if they see a ghost. Lily often looked at the level where a human face would be if someone was standing in the doorway of our family room.

"Does Dad know where his Mom's ring is, the one he mentioned last time? He wondered why I didn't have it."

"No. He doesn't know where it is." Darn.

"Are there any spirits in my house right now?"

"Your father-in-law was there with you when you first got on the call, but he isn't anymore.

"Gene!" I called out. No sign of him. "He probably took off because he didn't want to talk to us."

"That's probably about right given his personality." (Ha ha!)

I have kept the quarter my Dad gave me from beyond the grave—better than a mere penny from Heaven! But I wished I could communicate with him as easily as Morgan could.

At the end of August, Von and I both got on Zoom with Morgan again from our respective homes.

"Hi Renee, I haven't seen you for a while!" said Morgan.

Von asked some general questions about ghosts, and if our Dad was at her house. Morgan said he wasn't at either of our homes. "He buzzes around to everyone."

Then she asked, "Who is Jim?"

"That's my husband," said Von.

"He hangs around a lot with Jim."

Von started chalking that up to Dad teaching Jim a lot about building, and the two of them doing things together when he was alive.

"Where is Jim?" Morgan asked.

"He's at work—where Dad used to work. In fact, he was one of the four founders of the company, which started small and now has hundreds of workers. Our sister and his grandson also work there."

"He's with Jim."

We realized it made sense that Dad would hang out there

since he spent most of his working life at the company, and he used to go back and visit even after he retired.

"And you're the family that knows not to vote for Trump!" said Morgan, laughing. "I've never been asked that before. I suggest you try Zooming from the workplace to see if we can catch your Dad there."

Von and I weren't sure we could arrange that. Morgan Zoomed in the evening and we didn't think Dad would hang around after the workers had left—plus we didn't know if the company would let us come in and do a session.

When it was my turn, Morgan said "There are no spirits in your house right now, not your Dad, your father-in-law or any others. No negativity. No spirits. It's clear. Not like a lot of people in the squares today." That was the only time I had no spirits in all the sessions I Zoomed with Morgan.

She said about Dad, "Everything has to be done *his way*."

"That's true of a lot of men," I said.

"He checks to make sure things are being done right at work, especially since he was one of the owners. He's still invested in the place!"

I sought clarity about how I could have dreamt about my Dad even though he was Earthbound. "Did I sense him near and then dream about him because of that?"

"Exactly!"

"In the dream I said, "I've missed you so much since you've been gone," and he said "I'm not gone. I'm right here!""

"That was totally correct. He sure was telling the truth!"

"How do you see things on my property that you couldn't view on Zoom?" I asked.

"I get information through my spirit guides."

The more time I spent online with Morgan, the more I believed that she actually was psychic—but in a very specific way. She could only get psychic information that had to do with ghosts and what they saw and thought.

There were a lot of people on my October Zoom call with Morgan, and I was the second to the last person they called on (since I was a repeat). My Dad wasn't around, as I suspected, so I couldn't ask him any of the questions I had.

"He has a lot of places to go," said Morgan. "Does he have grandchildren too?"

"Yes. Lots."

"He probably stays a day or two in each place, plus he goes to his old workplace."

"Is there anyone else here?"

"A teenage boy was there, but he left about a half hour ago."

I thought, darn, that always happens because it takes so long to get to me on the Zoom calls. "What did he look like?"

"He looked to be about 18-20 years old. He had long, shaggy brown hair and was about six feet tall. He was wearing a jean jacket and Nike shoes with a swoosh on them. I think he died about three or four years ago. He had been standing by the green lights." (I had green Frankenstein lights around the front window.) "Have any teenagers died in the neighborhood lately?"

"I'm not aware of any."

"Have there been any car accidents nearby?"

I didn't know of any, but I wasn't too far from a freeway. I'd have to look that up. I wondered if the teenager saw my Halloween lights from outside and decided to come in and check out my decorations.

"I have an 1870s clock and the chime was off—it didn't match the time. But suddenly the chime became correct, on its own. Can you tell me anything about that?"

"Where did the clock come from?"

"It's from my Dad's side of the family. It belonged to his grandparents."

"Your Dad fixed the chime."

I had a question for Morgan about smudging. "Is it safe to

smudge with cats around?"

"Birds can't take smudging and older cats may not do well with it. You could put your cat in a carrier and take them outside when smudging. But you don't want to smudge or you'll keep your Dad away!"

"That's right!"

* * *

I kept dreaming of my father. In one dream, my Dad said, "There's no one in the room," and I felt he meant that there were no ghosts in the bedroom with me at that time.

In November, I sent Morgan a message when she was doing a YouTube Live session "I continue to dream of my Dad even though ghosts aren't supposed to be able to communicate with us via dreams. Is this just my psychic ability sensing him near, and then I dream of him?"

The moderator passed my message onto Morgan, and she responded.

"Exactly right," she said. "She does have that ability. I don't remember, or if I ever really knew, how long her father has been dead, but he's got a lot of energy for an older gentleman, let me tell you! And that man is determined—so that wouldn't surprise me. I think he's in her house enough where she's just picking up on it, and then she dreams about him."

I kept hoping I could connect with my father and ask him some questions, so I decided to Zoom with Morgan again in December, on the day of the winter solstice.

To my disappointment, Morgan said that neither my Dad nor father-in-law were around. (Darn!)

"However, the young man I saw last time is here again," she said. "It's been quite a while since we last Zoomed, so I don't think he's been around that whole time. He probably left and came back."

The last time she had thought the man looked about 19 or 20 but this time she thought he actually looked more like 25.

"He's wearing what looks like a motorcycle jacket." She paused. "He died in a motorcycle accident."

I started asking him questions aloud to see who he was and why he was here. "Are you here because of the animals?" I have some unusual snakes and I thought they might interest him, but I did not want to mention "snakes" because I knew that Morgan was terrified of them.

"He's making a gesture with his hand, holding it out and moving it back and forth, so it's not necessarily them." She showed me with his hand waffling back and forth, the universal sign for being noncommittal.

"He likes the animals—he's not mean to anyone," said Morgan. That was good to hear, since earlier a spirit had performed mischief with heat that endangered my reptiles.

"Did you pass on our street?" I asked the young ghost.

"He shook his head no."

"Did you die in Roseville?"

"That was a no."

"In Minnesota?"

"Yes."

"I'm getting the name Andrew. I think his name is Andrew."

She changed her mind when the ghost shook his head no.

"Apparently, he's looking for Andrew or knows him. Is your son named Andrew?

"No."

"Any of the neighbors?"

"None that I know of."

Morgan concentrated some more. "His name starts with a J...Jason or James.*"

The ghost shook his head yes to that.

"When did you die?" I asked him.

"He's holding up seven fingers."

"2007*?" I asked.

"Yes."

I let my husband know what we had learned about our

ghost. He did some online research and found only one man in his 20s who had died in a motorcycle accident in Minnesota the year the ghost had mentioned—and his name was Jason James Johnson*. I was excited because this guy checked all the boxes. His name wasn't Jason OR James, it was both!

An article on the motorcycle accident said that Jason had died on October 13, 2007*. He was born in 1979, so he was in his late twenties when he passed.

Of course, we still didn't know why he was visiting us. Did he know one of the neighbors and just popped into our house occasionally to see what was going on? Was he here because of the interesting animals? Was it because David watched sports a lot—and all the sports bars were closed because of COVID? Was it because David's a mystery novelist? (David said the guy wouldn't hang around just to watch him write because that's pretty boring.) Did he just like our quirky house, with all the antiquities, art, bones, skulls, crystals, antiques, and stuff?

I later told Jason aloud that I was fine with him being here as long as he didn't harm the animals or cause any problems.

*Name and dates have been changed to protect this sweet young man's family.

On Christmas Eve, 2020, we suddenly and unexpectedly lost David's mother, Pat. She died in an ambulance on the way to the hospital. It was a shock and cast a pall over our Christmas, already disturbingly celebrated in isolation because of Covid-19.

We knew that Pat would not have wanted to survive if she was left with a poor quality of life, which would have been likely given her suspected stroke. So, it was a blessing that she passed quickly, while she was still independent as she had always been, and always wanted to be. She lived and died on her own terms.

Since her husband had been waiting around for her since he

had died many years earlier, I wanted to know if they were both around now or if they had moved on—and if Pat had any preferences for her Memorial Service, which had been post-poned because of COVID. So I got on Zoom with Morgan again in February, shortly after what would have been Pat's 86th birthday.

As soon as the session started, I told Morgan about my mother-in-law's passing and asked if she sensed her or her husband around.

"I do not. Of course, they have other places they could go." Then she added, "Your young man is there, though."

I spoke over my shoulder toward where I thought he might be standing. "Are you this man?" I asked, as I held up a printout showing a photo of Jason, his headstone, and details about him from a memorial website.

"What's his last name?" Morgan asked.

I told her.

"Yes, that's him."

"Why is he hanging around here?" I asked. David and I were very curious about that.

"He likes what you do in your house," Morgan said. "Isn't your husband a writer?"

"Yes, he writes mystery novels. I'm also a writer. I like to go caving and scuba diving, do archery."

"There you go!" Morgan said.

I laughed; so he found us entertaining? Of course, I couldn't go caving or scuba diving during the pandemic. I couldn't carry my snakes in parades or show them at the Renaissance Festival, as usual. I couldn't visit historic towns and stay in haunted hotels. None of the interesting things I usually did were possi-ble. I *was* able to shoot arrows at a nearby park when it was warm out. But I thought it unlikely that we were entertaining enough for a young man.

"Could Jason have known your kids?"

"He was born in 1979, so he was older than my kids. They

were born much later."

"Are your kids around much?"

"They only come over briefly to pick up or drop off things and don't stay long; they don't want us catching COVID. They're both out working, and David and I work from home."

"What are their occupations?"

"My daughter is a horticulturist, and my son works for an investment bank."

"That's not it." She didn't think the ghost came in with one of them. "He must get enough energy from you."

I said, "I wear a protective charm so I don't think he can get it from me, just David."

"Is David always tired?"

"No." I had asked him about this before. But I later checked with him again and he confirmed that he wasn't particularly tired. I was probably more tired because I woke up every single night and sometimes had trouble returning to sleep.

"He is showing me a stethoscope in his ears," Morgan said.

I wondered if he had been going to medical school.

"He's making a cross with his two fingers, like this." Morgan showed her two forefingers crossing, in an X shape.

We tried to figure out what that meant. I suggested, "Rx?"

Morgan paused for a moment. Then she finally said, "No....x-ray technician. He's saying yes to that. He was an x-ray technician."

Morgan asked if his parents were dead, and I asked Jason.

"No, his parents are alive."

Morgan then asked about my parents.

"No, my Mom's alive, and you've seen my Dad."

"That's right." She was trying to figure out which parents the message was about. Finally she said it was about David's parents.

"Jason is saying your mother-in law and father-in-law are gone, that they both went into the light." I knew David would be very glad to hear that.

"However, your Dad's still around," she said. "He's stubborn."

"Well," I said, "my Mom's still alive and he's waiting for her. David's Dad was waiting for his Mom and she died, so he doesn't need to hang around anymore."

I looked back over my shoulder. "Thank you so much, Jason, for letting us know about Pat and Gene!"

"He's saluting you," said Morgan, copying his action by putting her hand at an angle to her forehead. "I think he's saying goodbye. He's going to leave soon."

My turn was over. I turned off my microphone and thanked Jason again for letting us know that Pat and Gene had gone into the light. I passed on the tip that Morgan tells everyone, so they're never trapped on Earth after they die. "If you are taking off and want to go into the light, just go to the nearest funeral home; when there's a wake or funeral, the light that leads to the other side will be there. You can walk in whenever you're ready."

I felt a connection and empathy for Jason and wished him the very best. I also felt very sad for his family, and knew how hard it must have been for his parents to lose him at such a young age.

I had to admit though, I wasn't sure the salute Morgan had demonstrated was an actual "goodbye." Wouldn't Jason have waved his hand in the universal "goodbye" gesture if that were the case? The salute could have simply been an acknowledgment of my gratitude and meant, "Glad I could help."

I wouldn't know for sure until I Zoomed with Morgan again in the future.

ROAD TRIP TO
MEET THE MEDIUM

"The Supernatural is the Natural, just not yet understood."
—*Elbert Hubbard*

When COVID vaccines arrived, the world started to open up—and I planned a visit to meet the woman behind the ghosts on Zoom.

My sister picked me up at 6 am on Midsummer Day—also the Full Moon—which seemed appropriate for a road trip to see Morgan. We stopped only twice briefly, during the nearly 12-hour drive, finally arriving at our motel.

The next morning, we drove to meet Morgan and her husband at a metaphysical shop. When we saw a car drive up with a ghost-themed license plate and a decal featuring the Ghostbusters ghost with a null sign over it, we knew exactly who had arrived.

Morgan said that if Mercury Retrograde hadn't ended shortly before we drove out, she would have told us not to come. (Mercury Retrograde is a period that occurs several times a year, when the planet appears to be moving backwards, and all kinds of things are reputed to go wrong, including travel.)

We had a great time talking about Morgan's amazing adventures over lunch. After we had finished eating, I asked her if my Dad had come with us and she said, "No—but he could still show up." She asked if I had put a note up for him at home and I said yes, a week or two ago, asking him to come with us, and so did Von. I was disappointed that he hadn't come. Morgan thought he would come for my birthday (which was two days away, still during our trip).

"He wasn't around the last few times we Zoomed," I said.

"I did get the sense the last time I talked with him that he might be getting tired of answering questions."

"Is anyone else with us?" I knew Von was hoping Morgan would mention Gryphon, her beloved standard poodle, who had recently passed. But the earthbound spirits we had expected to show up did not—while unexpected ghosts did.

Morgan said there was an old woman with Von. "Her name is Edith." Von asked if the name was Gladys (her mother-in-law, who had passed). But Morgan said "No, her name is Edith Hu...something, the last name starts with an H."

She also got the number 907, but didn't know what it meant.

Von said, "That's the number of my address!"

Morgan said the ghost woman said that is *her* home—that is where she lives.

I asked Von, "What was the name of the woman who owned the house before you?"

Von looked stunned. She said Edith Huntington* had lived in the house, which was built in the 1950s by the government for her son. He had been injured during basic training for the Korean War and ended up in a wheelchair. She thought Edith might have gone into a nursing home after her son had died.

"How long have you lived there?" Morgan asked.

"Since 1996," Von said.

Von had always wondered if her house was haunted because of some occurrences that had happened there—and it turned out her instincts were right! She had apparently been sharing her house with Edith for decades.

Morgan said she spoke to the woman telepathically, and Edith was shocked that Morgan could see her. When she tried to ask the ghost a question, she fled. Morgan said "I would like to see if I can help Edith go into the light tomorrow at the carousel museum."

* *Name changed to protect her family.*

The next day, we drove to the haunted Merry-Go-Round Museum. Almost all of the visitors were local. We had traveled the furthest distance to come to the event.

We went into the museum, and saw a bunch of chairs set up to the right of a huge carousel at the center of a big open space. Most of them were filled, and we learned there had been a lot of walk-ins. I wanted to sit in the mostly empty front row, but Von did not, so we sat in the second row—and luckily no one sat in front of us to obstruct our view.

Morgan gave a presentation about ghosts and answered questions. She let people know which earthbound spirits were currently near them.

Once more, our Dad was not there as we had hoped. I was very disappointed.

But Morgan told Von she had TWO ghosts with her now, Edith and a man. She said, "His name is Arnie Johnson.*"

Von said, "He died recently."

"In 2018," Morgan said.

He was the father of Von's neighbor, Peter Johnson.* Von wondered what her neighbor Mary,* his daughter-in-law, would think when she told her. She had informed Mary about her impending trip to see Morgan. It made me think that the ghost had overhead the conversation and decided to come down with us, maybe so Morgan could help him cross over.

According to Morgan, Arnie said, "Karen* doesn't believe anything!"

Von said that Karen was his ex-wife, who may have remarried. That made me wonder if Arnie had been trying to get her attention and she had refused to believe it was him, or that ghosts were real.

Morgan said, "He visits David's house, too." He gave a name, "Wandra.*"

Von said "That's another neighbor; Eileen Wandra* is very elderly and lives with David, her son."

Morgan said she would send both Edith and Arnie into the light. Unfortunately, we could not see her do it and since she talks to them telepathically, we didn't know when it happened. But she later told us she had been successful. So, Von's house was now clear.

Morgan then said that Gladys was around Von a lot. "She's watching out for her son." (Von's husband, Jim.)

*Names have been changed to protect their families.

When I asked about demons, Morgan said, "Demons are overrated." She had encountered very few, even though many Ghost TV shows seemed to claim they were everywhere. She said there are plenty of negative people (like Hitler and serial killers), but not a lot of demons. That was good to hear.

GHOST GUIDE

"The house ghost is usually a harmless and well-meaning creature...
It brings good luck to those who live with it."
—William Butler Yeats

A Quick Cheat Sheet on Ghosts

Here's what I've observed, experienced, read, and heard from Morgan and other experts, that I believe is true:

- Earthbound spirits are the spirits of those who have died on Earth. We usually call them ghosts. Most people move on to the light (the other side) after death, but atheists, those who have killed themselves. or have committed serious crimes, may hang around for fear of receiving punishment. Others stick around to watch over loved ones—or to spy on them (if they're nosy)—or for entertainment (going to ballgames, theater, traveling) until they have had enough and are ready to reunite with their loved ones on the other side.
- Ghosts usually know they're dead. They can't do anything physically, can't pick things up, can't eat, don't sleep, people can't see them, etc. Unless they've had a

mental disability in life, they can figure it out pretty darned quickly. So, forget about the myth that a ghost "doesn't know they're dead."

- Some people are so in love with a location or with a particular possession that after they die, they "attach" themselves to it—basically sticking close to it. They're not stuck, as some living people think. They're just stubborn! Ghosts can usually go wherever they want.

- Because they are pure energy, ghosts can affect electronics of all kinds. They will turn on and off pretty much anything that runs on energy: lights, computers, TVs, sound systems. Some ghosts have enough power to move objects—such as those at the location where I and many others have experienced poltergeist activity.

- Many men stick around and wait for their wives to pass so they can go into the light together. (That happened with both my Dad and my father-in-law.) I thought they were being gentlemen, wanting to escort their wives into Heaven. But David said they probably think they have a better chance of getting into Heaven if their wives are with them; he asked me to get him in. (Ha ha ha!)

- Relatives will come through your home, but don't usually stay for long because they don't want to sap your energy or make you sick (which is why my Dad was only occasionally around). Most of the time, the ghosts who stay full time in your home are strangers.

- Child ghosts prefer to hang around with live kids or other ghost kids. They love the toys they find near living children. They also like that small children can often see them (while most adults cannot), so they can talk to them and become their playmates. Parents may erroneously think that their children are just talking to "imaginary friends" when they're actually having conversations with ghosts.

- Adult ghosts don't usually hang around in groups together in a house. That's probably because they need to take energy from the living to maintain themselves—and when multiple ghosts gather in a location, they're all competing for a limited supply of energy. However, places with lots of living people, such as hotels, theaters and shopping malls, can support multiple ghosts.

- Animals are more likely than people to see ghosts. My cat Lily will frequently stare at the doorway of one of our rooms at human face level as if she's looking at a person who is standing there. When I described to my vet the experience that David and I had of our deceased cat rubbing against our legs, she asked if our new cat Lily acted like she saw another cat. She said that cats and dogs can definitely see ghosts. The vet described the behaviors Lily might exhibit if she saw a ghost cat, such as hissing or arching her back while staring at a blank space. (Lily clearly didn't; I wasn't surprised since both David and I felt our previous cat had been saying good-bye and hadn't stuck around.) If a ghost is already in your house when you bring in a new animal, they will often think that the ghost belongs there and may have no problem with it. However, if the ghost shows up after the pet, the animal may be upset by the new visitor—especially if they tease or harass the animal.

- Earthbound spirits look the same as they did when they died. However, their "body" is instantly whole when they die. They no longer have any missing parts or feel physical pain. They cannot change their appearance the way people who have gone into the light can (who can make themselves look younger, or however they want). Ghosts do not become spiritually evolved or know more than what they can observe by wandering around unseen. They can't predict the future or pick winning lottery numbers!

- Some people think cemeteries are spooky—although I

have to admit, I love old gravestones and ancient cemeteries, and often wander around them, taking photos.
However, ghosts do not usually hang around cemeteries
because they need to take energy from living people. Instead, they spend a lot of time at places where people
congregate: theaters, bars, restaurants, shopping centers,
stadiums, ball parks, concerts, etc. That's also why
you'll find more ghosts in cities than in the country. Los
Angeles, Chicago, New York, any big city, will have lots
of spirits. Usually, a house will just have one or two
ghosts, not a bunch.

- Places like dental offices and hospitals, where intense
  emotions such as fear or anxiety are aroused, are especially attractive to ghosts. Extreme emotions give ghosts
  a bigger boost of energy. That's why some mean-spirited
  ghosts deliberately try to scare people—for the bigger
  energy payoff. Other ghosts will try to make couples
  fight—then suck up the energy boost when emotions run
  high. Unfortunately, that's why people who live in
  haunted houses will sometimes split up. Staying calm is
  the best way to disappoint these troublesome ghosts.
  THEY ONLY HAVE THE POWER YOU GIVE
  THEM.

- Never use a Ouija board. It's like opening your front
  door and inviting every stranger who happens by to
  come inside. You have no control over who shows up,
  and are likely to attract opportunistic, lower-level entities or ghosts who enjoy causing mischief and misery.
  Seances can be just as problematic.

- Try to avoid anything that can attract negative entities
  (and problems) such as dabbling in black magic, drug or
  alcohol abuse, deep hatred toward anyone, overwhelming anger, blowout fights or arguments, physical abuse,
  violence, etc. Murder and suicide sites may attract darker spirits, and if you visit, they could follow you home.

Dark entities will even try to influence someone who is depressed to commit suicide. If you have suicidal thoughts, seek help immediately! Basically, if something feels dark or negative, it has the potential to draw more negativity and the entities that feed on this. Avoid those situations!

- Extreme actions such as murder, suicide, rape or physical abuse can sometimes blow open a portal in the place where they occurred. A portal is a doorway that allows negative spirits to enter the space. Many different spirits can enter and exit the portal, although only one at a time may be able to emerge. These ghosts are typically the worst types of criminals, who may have been executed for their crimes; they are afraid to go into the light for fear they will be sent to Hell. Because of their negative nature, they will tend to instigate fights, break things, and in general, create mayhem and nastiness wherever they go. To prevent them from coming through the portal, you will need to sage your home thoroughly and regularly, until you can get an expert to come over and close the portal. If you know where the portal is located, you can simply sage the room where it resides; do it often. This will discourage ghosts from coming out.

Ghost Energy

Every living creature on this planet obtains energy from eating food. Whether we eat plants or other animals, we take in calories, which power our bodies. Even at rest, the average human produces about 100 watts of power. A person running at top speed can put out over 2,000 watts.

Since the first law of thermodynamics states that "energy can neither be created nor destroyed" what happens to our energy when we die?

There is more and more evidence that our spirit is composed of conscious energy—and it exits our body when that physical shell ceases to function.

For example: People have captured photographs of white lights or streaks that suggest a luminous energy where ghosts are reputed to be present. Ghosts can very easily mess with electronics—turning on and off lights, TVs, toys or computers—even when they're not plugged in or the batteries have been removed. They can initiate "phantom" telephones calls; no voice answers when you pick up and the call may come from the cell phone of a deceased person or a line that's not in service. Ghosts can burn out or abruptly explode lightbulbs, instantly drain batteries, and short out electronic devices. They can record audible messages (EVPs) on digital recorders that can only be heard when the recording is played back. They can create words and sentences out of electronic "white noise" machines. They can suck the heat out of a room on a hot summer day so the temperature abruptly drops (without air-conditioning).

Ghost hunters often use EMF meters that measure electro-magnetic energy to confirm that ghosts are present (after first making sure there's no normal electronic source for EMF in the area); temporary spikes in energy can indicate a spirit passing through.

Because ghosts are spirits, they cannot eat food to maintain their energy—they have to get it from somewhere else. They primarily draw energy from living human beings. That's why people who have a ghost in their house may feel tired or have minor health issues. It's not necessarily that the ghost is trying to hurt them. The earthbound spirit just needs to tap energy to maintain their existence and activity—and that may weaken the living person.

However, some selfish ghosts will try to boost the emotional level of the humans they haunt, deliberately instigating terror, fighting, anger, drama or outbursts, because that raises the humans' energy level, giving the earthbound spirits more to feed on. A ghost may deliberately change the dynamic of the family in a negative way for their own gain.

A good way to shut that down is to deny ghosts the hyper-emotional energy they crave. Do NOT be afraid of them. Stay calm. Do NOT get upset with those you live with. Remember that you love them.

You have way more power than any ghost. Never forget that. (The ghosts won't.)

MANAGING YOUR GHOSTS

*"Some people go to mediums to bring them into contact
with the spirit world, but most go to bartenders."*
—Evan Esar

Rule Out the Normal Before Assuming Paranormal

If you have experienced incidents in your home or had odd
sensations or feelings that make you think you may have an
earthbound spirit hanging around, first try to rule out other
possibilities. Could you have mice in the walls, a raccoon
walking on the roof, or bats in the attic? Could a neighbor next
door or a bird on the window be causing those pounding or
knocking sounds? (Birds sometimes peck at the old trim on our
house and they are very noisy!)

Check your carbon monoxide detector because symptoms of
carbon monoxide poisoning can mimic some people's physical
reactions to the presence of a ghost, such as headache, weak-
ness, dizziness, nausea or vomiting, shortness of breath, and
confusion. Get out of the house if you experience this! Have the
CO levels checked.

We are all exposed to natural and man-made electromagnetic
fields in our lives, from the sun, microwaves, cell phones, TVs,
power mains, and electronics around us. Like carbon monoxide

poisoning, high EMF levels can result in symptoms similar to those of a serious haunting: insomnia, headache, depression, tiredness, poor concentration, memory problems, dizziness, irritability, anxiety, nausea, skin burning/tingling, and loss of appetite leading to weight loss.

When ghost hunters use EMF meters to detect the presence of earthbound spirits, readings will usually vary—there may be a spike in one spot in the home that disappears as the ghost moves away. If a location has high EMF levels due to electronic issues, the EMF meter will register a number that stays consistent, not go up and down as you remain in the same spot.

Your Perspective on the Paranormal

Recent polls have found that most Americans believe in ghosts—but most are not frightened by these spirits. On the other hand, some are so scared of ghosts that they have full-blown phasmophobia—extreme anxiety or terror that can be triggered by the mere mention of something supernatural. They may also develop related fears of the darkness or being alone and can become too scared to go to the bathroom at night.

Unfortunately, unscrupulous ghosts can prey on these people's fears by making their presence known in a dramatic way, triggering a burst of terror that they can then feed on. If they get the reward of that big emotional response, they will keep acting up, because it works!

If you're afraid of ghosts, you will want to get rid of them. Fortunately, there are actions you can take to make them want to leave your home. (We'll get to those shortly.)

On the other hand, if you're not afraid of ghosts, then like me, you may not mind sharing your home with them. However, since they can drain your energy, you may want to protect yourself so you don't feel tired all the time or get minor illnesses more often than you should.

There are lots of tactics and tools you can use to manage your ghosts. You can make them settle down or even banish them, if they're causing serious problems. Be confident, firm, and unafraid as you take action. You have more power than they do.

Yes, they're invisible—which may feel like a super-power to us—but they can't do most of the things we can. Although some ghosts can move objects, it takes a lot of energy and most of them do it rarely, if ever.

One caveat before you jump in: if the signs suggest you may be dealing with a demon, get help with that! Demons are dark entities that were never human and can't be dealt with in the same way as ghosts. Interestingly, 54% of Republicans believe in demons, but only 37% of Democrats do (according to a recent poll).

Fortunately, demons are much rarer than the paranormal shows on TV suggest. Mean-spirited ghosts are usually responsible for the activity attributed to demons. I will discuss demons in more depth later in the book.

Blessings

To dispel or quiet ghosts, many people start by asking their priest, minister, or spiritual leader to come to their home and bless it. If the prayers are done in a loving and respectful way, this blessing may encourage the ghosts to behave themselves.

You can also bless yourself with holy water for purification and protection from evil. Catholics usually make the sign of the cross with holy water, applying it to the forehead (while saying "In the name of the Father..."), solar plexus ("...and of the Son..."), left shoulder ("and of the Holy..."), then right shoulder ("...Spirit. Amen"). Interesting enough, "Holy Ghost" was once the most prevalent name in the Catholic Church for the third person in the Trinity.

Just don't get carried away with the holy water. If you skip getting a blessing by a spiritual leader and instead get a bottle of holy water and start throwing it everywhere, that can actually anger the ghosts. It's like you are saying that they are evil, demonic beings that are repelled by holy water—which is pretty insulting. Instead of settling down, they may act up even more, just to prove they're not evil entities who are terrified of holy water—or you.

Smudging

Smudging—the burning of purifying herbs to dispel negative energy from people, places, or objects—has become the go-to way most people deal with hauntings. There are instructions and videos all over the web, and I've included how-to steps in the next section. Methods vary. Some say to start at the top of a house/building, while others say to begin at the bottom and then work your way through the rest of the structure. Some say to smudge in a clockwise direction, others say the opposite. Some say open a window while you smudge, others (such as Morgan) say to keep all windows closed for two hours after you have finished, to give the smoke time to permeate everything before you air out the house.

One thing all practitioners agree on: don't miss a corner or a closet. Don't forget the basement, the attic, and the garage if it's attached. Wherever you don't smudge is where the ghost will hide out until you're done to avoid the effects of the smoke, and the whole process will have been in vain.

I don't think it matters so much at which end of the house you start or what direction you walk as long as you do a thorough job.

Sage is the most popular plant burned for smudging smoke and reputedly the most powerful. Usually, you will find white sage premade into "sticks" of bundled herbs that can be lit on one end.

You can also try palo santo. I love the smell of that ancient wood; however, many sources say it is not as effective as sage at banishing ghosts.

Be very careful about where you obtain your smudging ingredients. It's best to get them from Native American or indigenous peoples who harvest them in a respectful and sustainable way.

Although Celtic druids and witches in Europe burned sage too, most of the sage sold in North America is white sage native to our continent and sacred to the peoples who lived here for centuries. It must be used with deep respect for their culture and also for the spirits you want to calm with the herb.

Never harvest white sage from land that is not yours. You can grow your own sage for personal use. (I have grown beautiful tricolor sage in pots in my front yard.) Then make bundles by wrapping the sage with string, as described further below. These will be ready to burn when the sage has dried.

How to Smudge

- Gather your sage bundle or palo santo stick, a large feather, matches or candle, and an abalone shell or other container. Close the windows of the home or building you intend to clear.
- Light the end of the sage bundle or palo santo stick. Let it burn for a little while and then blow it out. Smoke will start rising.
- Hold the abalone shell under the smoking bundle or stick. Use the feather to fan out the smoke from the end.
- Start at the top of your house (such as your attic). Fan smoke along all the walls and corners of that floor.
- Proceed down to the next floor, sending smoke everywhere, including into closets and cupboards.

- If the sage or palo santo stops smoking, relight it. Continue smudging from the location where it went out. (Note that palo santo may be harder to keep lit than sage. If it goes out frequently, you may want to use a candle to keep relighting it.)
- Continue sending smoke thoroughly into each corner and area of each floor of the house or building as you proceed downward, including the basement and any attached buildings, such as a garage.
- Do a thorough job! The one place you don't smudge is where a ghost may hide to avoid the effects of the smoke.
- When you're finished, place the end of the smoking stick or bundle into a bowl of sand to douse it.

CAUTION: If you have asthma or a respiratory condition, talk to your doctor before smoking up your home. Also, send young children to Grandma's house or outside with your partner while you smudge. It's best to put pets outside, as well.

Some people think a single smudging will banish ghosts. That is NOT usually the case. Smudging simply makes ghosts lethargic so things will quiet down. However, after a while, often just a couple of weeks, they will regain their energy and may start acting up again. Smudge the entire house or building again to dampen their spirits.

If you want to permanently get rid of ghosts, you may need to repeat smudging your space every 10 days to keep them lethargic, so eventually, they get fed up and leave. It's a simple matter of persistently making your home less hospitable to them!

If you just want to keep ghosts from being a nuisance in a particular room, such as a bedroom, you can smudge that room frequently instead of doing the whole house.

If you do not have access to premade white sage smudge sticks or want to make your own purifying tools instead of purchasing them, you can use other herbs to make your own bundle for smoking a room or home. (These may not be as powerful as traditional white sage.)

How To Make Your Own Smudge Stick

- Gather a bunch of sprigs of fresh sage from your garden or a farmer's market. You can also include other powerful herbs, such as rosemary, lavender, juniper, cedar or mugwort.
- Tie the base of the stems together with cotton string or embroidery thread, leaving one end of the string or thread quite long.
- Start wrapping upward from the base of the herbs at a 45-degree angle with the long end of the string/thread. Keep going all the way to the top of the bundle of sprigs.
- Then start wrapping in the opposite direction, back down toward the bottom of the sprigs, still at a 45-degree angle, repeatedly crossing over the string/thread you wrapped going upward, creating right angles.
- When you reach the base of the stems, knot the string/thread again where you originally tied the base of the sprigs together.
- You can trim off the stems at the bottom and any protruding leaves, if you desire.
- Let the bundle of herbs dry thoroughly before using.

Other herbs that have been used for warding off evil or cleansing a space that you could also incorporate into your bundle: peppermint, thyme, dill, nettle, rue and oregano. Some people also add flower petals, such as rose petals. (The rose is considered to have the highest vibration of any flower. The higher the frequency of vibration, the lighter and more positive an object or being feels.)

* * *

Smudge Sprays

You can buy a "smudge spray" marketed as an alternative to smudging for use in locations where you can't burn sage (such as a workplace or dorm room). Basically, these sprays are powered by essential oils from sage, palo santo, and/or other herbs known for their cleansing power. You can also make your own smudge spray, tailored to your preferences.

One caveat: many people say sprays are not as effective as genuine smudging. They may raise the vibration/mood of the room, but may not make your ghost feel lethargic like burning sage does.

How to make your own smudge spray

- You will need an 8-ounce spray bottle, witch hazel or inexpensive vodka, sea salt, water, and the essential oils you want to include, such as palo santo and/or white sage, plus any others you want to add, possibly lavender, rosemary, cedar, or rose.
- Pour ½ cup of warm water into the bottle.
- Add 2 teaspoons of sea salt. Stir it into the warm water until it dissolves.
- Pour ½ cup of witch hazel or vodka into the bottle.
- Add 15 or more drops of each essential oil you wish to include.
- If you love crystals, you can add a small, charged piece of clear quartz, amethyst, or rose quartz to give your

spray a boost. (Don't add just any crystal since some dissolve in water. Do a little research first to make sure your favorite stone isn't toxic or water soluble.)

- Screw on the top and shake the bottle well.
- Mist the air of the room you wish to cleanse. You can also lightly spray an object, or even yourself. Mist the air in front of you and walk through it—or spray it above your head and let it settle on you. (Don't spray it in your eyes!)

Florida Water

Florida Water cologne has been around since 1808. The name was meant to suggest the Fountain of Youth, which was supposedly located in Florida, now ironically home to lots of elderly people. The cologne has an alcohol base and contains essential oils such as lavender, lemon, orange, and other flowers and spices.

Many people think Florida Water can keep negative energies away, which is why it has long been a staple in folk magic practices.

You can mist the air in your home, or any room that feels negative, with Florida water to raise the vibration. I like to spray the air above my bed before I go to sleep.

Will that help calm your ghosts? Maybe. Maybe not.

If you like the scent, as I do, at least it might make you feel happier.

White Candles

Some people believe burning a white candle can discourage ghosts. There is positive energy in the pure white color of the candle and in the bright light of the flame (dispelling darkness).

You can boost its power by adding a couple of drops of essential oils, such as sage, palo santo or rosemary, to the top of the candle before lighting it. You can also buy candles already infused with protective essential oils (but expect to pay more for the convenience).

Since these candles will spread aroma around your home, choose an essential oil scent you like. Make sure to keep all candles out of the reach of children and animals—and never leave them unattended.

Some people recommend putting a glass of water next to a white candle to attract spirits. As you light the candle, say a prayer and ask that the spirit cross over to the other side. Let the candle burn until it goes out.

Are ghosts supposed to use the brightness of the flame as a doorway to the white light that takes them to the other side? I don't know how that is supposed to work—or if it even does—but it might be fun to try it and see what happens.

Sea Salt

Salt has been used for cleansing, preserving, and protecting purposes throughout history. Sea salt is less processed than table salt and for that reason, seems to hold more power. Its white color (like the candle) represents purity and light. Plus, salt is a crystal and many people think crystals hold special powers.

Add more power to your sea salt by taking it to your priest, minister or spiritual leader and asking them to bless it. Blessed sea salt is particularly potent.

Blessed or not, sea salt can be used to protect you from spirits in a variety of ways:

- Sprinkle newly purchased antiques or used items with a little sea salt before heading home, to keep a ghost from coming with you.

- Fill a spray bottle with water and add a couple of table-spoons of sea salt. To make ghosts keep their distance, mist the air and walk through it or spray the mist above your head and let it settle on you.
- If you have been at a haunted location, mist the inside of your vehicle with your salt spray before driving home to keep ghosts from hitching a ride.
- Pour a line of sea salt across each entrance to your home to keep ghosts at bay. You can also do this at the entrance to your hotel room when you're traveling. (Hopefully the ghost is not already in the room when you arrive!)
- Place a bowl of sea salt in each room of your home or in the corners of rooms where you want to cleanse the energy and calm spirits.
- Purchase or make sea salt soap and use it in the bath or shower to cleanse yourself of any attachments or negative energy.
- You can even go big, and sprinkle sea salt around the entire outside perimeter of your house—or around the boundaries of your whole yard.
- Consider buying sea salt in bulk to save money. It's great for cooking too!

Black Crystals

Many people attribute healing, protective, or spiritual properties to crystals, which are minerals or gems with atoms or molecules arranged in a regular, orderly way.

The most common mineral on earth is quartz, a crystal with molecules of silicon dioxide arranged in a lattice. Another crystal that has ions arranged in a lattice (sodium and chloride this time) is ordinary table salt. Other crystals can have different molecular patterns.

So, which ones are best for repelling or calming ghosts?

All black stones are considered protective—such as shungite, hematite, obsidian, onyx, jet, magnetite, and black or smoky quartz. But black tourmaline is the hands-down favorite. It is reputed to repel negative energy and also protect people from psychic attacks. It probably won't send your ghosts packing, though.

Here's how to use your black tourmaline (and other black crystals):

- Carry a small piece with you, in your pocket or purse.
- Wear a pendant or jewelry made of black tourmaline. (I wear a bracelet of black tourmaline almost every day.)
- Keep a piece of black tourmaline on your nightstand near your bed, or under your pillow.
- Place black tourmaline crystals in each corner of a room with ghost activity.
- Make a house-wide protective grid by placing black tourmaline at each corner of the home.
- Place black tourmaline at each entrance to the home.

Iron

Long before the Iron Age and the smelting of iron ore, ancient peoples found iron in meteorites that had fallen to earth. One example: scientists analyzed 5,000-year-old iron beads found in Egypt and determined the metal came from meteorites.

Because it had come from the sky, people thought iron had powerful supernatural properties. Marvelous artifacts were created out of this magical gift from the gods. In very short supply before smelting began thousands of years later, iron was initially reserved for royalty.

Since iron was originally created via fusion in the heart of giant stars and spewed out in the super-powerful explosions of supernovas, maybe they weren't too far wrong in thinking it miraculous.

For centuries, iron was believed to protect against evil spirits, ghosts, witches, fairies, and djinn (also called genies). Children's beds were made of iron to protect them from being snatched by evil supernatural beings. Iron horseshoes were placed over doors to prevent evil beings from entering the house (and later, to bring luck). Cast iron or iron ore chunks were laid at the threshold to prevent a supernatural invasion.

Some people still believe iron can provide such protection. They may use traditional iron amulets such as railroad spikes, fire irons, knives, shears, nails, or tools to protect a home by placing them over the doorways.

In a recent ghost-hunting television episode, a paranormal investigation group claimed that they were able to trap a ghost in a room by putting iron railroad spikes over the doorframe.

Others have suggested putting iron nails, shavings, or filings into an empty glass jar by each door of a house to protect people inside from curses and dark energy.

I'm very skeptical about the power of iron to repel ghosts, but it could be fun to try this ancient spirit repellant. Make sure to use pure iron and not steel, which is not reputed to hold the same power.

If you are being bothered by ghosts at night, put iron over the doorway to your bedroom when you're sure no entities are present. See if it keeps them from annoying you—and if it works, please let me know!

SOUND

"Everything in life is vibration"
—Albert Einstein

You may actually be able to soothe yourself, the energy of your home—and potentially any spirits present—with something as simple as sound.

Everything in the universe is vibrating, oscillating, resonating at some frequency. This includes rocks, animals, trees, people—everything on earth. It's happening at a level that we cannot perceive, so things will appear to be still even though they are constantly in motion at an atomic or subatomic level. What we see as solid matter is actually created by vibrations of various underlying fields.

Everything is moving. Energy is everywhere.

Interestingly, when things vibrating at different frequencies are brought together, they often "synch" in what is described as "spontaneous self-organization." This is similar to how, when a bunch of fireflies of some species gather, they start to flash in sync.

This suggests we may be able to use sound to modify our frequency or energy levels—and perhaps those of the ghosts in our homes, who are pure energy.

Many of us are already doing this unawares, by playing our

favorite songs. We've experienced the power of music (sound vibrations) to change our emotional level (also a form of vibration). Music can uplift, make us feel happy, sad, wistful, energized—all via vibrations.

Sound can help us reset a vibration that feels "off" or raise the surrounding vibration level.

Some people believe that ringing bells can clear the energy in a room. Others swear by singing bowls. Here are some sound techniques you can try to add positive energy to your space and perhaps make your ghosts less bellicose.

In each case, move around your space as you make the sound, much as you would walk throughout your home while smudging.

Singing Bowls

These were traditionally made of hand-forged bronze in Tibet, which can still be found as antiques. But you can also choose new brass bowls hand-hammered in Nepal (like mine) or crystal singing bowls. Each bowl is tuned to a specific note, often associated with one of the chakras. To play the bowl, simply hit it with the accompanying wooden striker, then run the striker around the outside of the bowl in circles to sustain the note while the bowl rests on your palm with fingers outstretched. I personally find that the singing bowl is very soothing. It can put your mind in a relaxed and meditative mode, thus raising your vibration. I would not be surprised if it has the same effect on earthbound spirits.

Bells

Ringing a bell can bring positive energy to your space. You can choose antique bells, such as Tibetan bells, or you can use crystal bells—or any bell that has a sound that appeals to you. I have bells that have been gifted to me, one I found buried in the ground, and others I inherited. They all have different pitches. If you're curious about what note your bell rings, you can go online and strike the notes of a virtual piano to determine which matches your bell's sound (That's what I did). The most important thing is to select a bell that has a sound you love and makes you feel good.

Drums

There is a reason that drumming has been a part of many rituals and festivities around the world for thousands of years. The rhythmic beat of a drum mimics the heartbeat. It's primal. It engages your body (you get to hit something!) and recent research has shown drumming can relieve stress, improve heart health, and boost happiness. It can also speed healing, help the immune system, relieve anxiety, grief, fatigue, and depression. Of course, like other sounds, it can change the vibration of a location. You don't need a particular instrument or special training to hit a drum. Think of the little kids who get toy drums and have a blast. So can you! Try walking around your home drumming and see what I mean. (I have a bodhran and took lessons; it's a lot of fun!)

Music and Chanting

Many people love to chant ancient Sanskrit words or phrases such as "Om mani padme hum" or "Tat tvam asi." You can also listen to beautiful Gregorian chants. It's easy to find beautiful chant videos on YouTube. Another option is to play your favorite piece of uplifting music, whether that's Beethoven's Fifth, or the theme to a joyful movie. Let the sound fill your space—and your heart (without rattling the windows and angering your neighbors).

* * *

Rhythm Sticks

Rhythm sticks are a pair of wooden sticks that you hit together to make a sound. You can buy a set—or you can get them for free: just go outdoors and find two sturdy sticks; snap or cut them to your desired length. You can choose twigs that still have the bark on them, or search for sticks that have lost their bark and are smooth. Hit your sticks together to make sure you like the sound they make and that they are sturdy enough to use again and again. Sticks made of different woods and of varying diameters will create different sounds. Other options: cut a wooden dowel to the lengths you want and sand the edges. You can also try chopsticks (but these tend to be rather quiet).

Banging Pots/Pans

Some people swear by the tradition of loudly banging on pots or pans to drive out ghosts or dark spirits. It is a New Year's practice among some cultures. But you can try it whenever you want to calm or banish ghosts. Try opening a window or door and firmly telling them to leave as you drive them crazy with all of the noise. Maybe threatening to make a racket regularly will impel your ghosts to find a new home!

Clapping

If you don't have any of the resources mentioned above, but want to change the vibration of your space, just use your hands. Clap your hands together over and over as you move throughout your space. Do it with the speed and volume that feels right to you. You may choose a specific rhythmic pattern that appeals to you or has meaning to you (such as 1. 2. 1,2,3.) If you want, sing as you go, clapping in rhythm with the song. This lets you immediately clear out negativity without spending the time or money to assemble tools.

For maximum impact, remember to use each of these techniques as you move around your home from top to bottom, sending the sound waves through every room.

Divine Light

You can protect yourself—and loved ones—with a visualization and affirmation to keep what is spiritually and psychically negative away from you.

Close your eyes. Take a slow, deep breath, and hold it for a few seconds. Then exhale the air even more slowly than you inhaled it. Pause for a few seconds. Repeat this process three times. Slowing your breathing will automatically begin to calm your nervous system.

In your mind's eye, imagine a sphere of bright white light surrounding you. The white light can appear brilliant or sparkly; it doesn't matter. Let the light completely fill you and the inside of the sphere. As you visualize the light, say aloud or in your mind an affirmation such as:

"I am protected from all harm by the white light of Divine Love."

"I protect myself with the white light of God's love."

"The power of light and love protects me now and always."

"I shield myself from harm with the white light of Divine Love."

"God's light and love protect me."

"Divine love and light protect me from all negative energy and entities. I am safe."

"I enfold myself in the white light of God's love and protection."

Or create your own affirmation of protection that connects to the white light.

You can also recite a favorite prayer as you encircle yourself with the white light—such as the "Prayer for Protection" that has been popular around the world since it was written by James Dillet Freeman in the 1940s. (Here, "me" has been substituted for "us.")

The Light of God surrounds me.
The love of God enfolds me.
The Power of God protects me.
The Presence of God watches over me.
Wherever I am, God is.

Sit in the white light and feel the Divine Presence. Know that you are loved and protected.

If you don't believe in God, you can still imagine a shield of white light surrounding you, but instead appeal to whatever positive power in which you place your trust. (I presume if you're reading this book, you do believe there is a realm beyond the physical.)

Here are more light protection techniques you can use. Add

the affirmation you prefer in each case.

- When you take a shower, imagine that white or golden light is pouring down on you, cleansing you of everything you want to shed, whether that's negative energy or unwanted attachments.
- Place your fingertips on the center of the top of your head. Now pull your hands downward as you visualize yourself pulling a curtain of light over your entire body, all the way to the ground. This light can be whatever color you prefer. Set an intention to shield yourself from all harm and negativity.
- Visualize a column of white or golden light coming down from the sky like a spotlight to completely envelop you as it proceeds downward toward the center of the Earth. Stand in this powerful light and feel protected.
- Imagine you are pulling on a long cloak of white light that shimmers with iridescent strands of color. The hood covers your head, and the cloak encloses your body in light and protection. Feel safe, secure, and loved within your cloak of light and love.
- When you drive anywhere, imagine a sphere of white light around your vehicle and say this or another protective affirmation: "I shield my car and myself with the white light of God's love and protection."
- You can use the same white light technique and affirmation to protect your loved ones wherever they are. (e.g. "I surround my son with the white light of God's love and protection." or another affirmation.)

Speak Your Power

Your words have power.

If ghosts are waking you up, scaring your pet, or otherwise bothering you, take charge. It's YOUR home, not theirs. They were supposed to move on to the other side, and not loiter around the material world endlessly.

Stand up for yourself in the place where they are most active. Be firm, confident, strong, and unafraid. Tell them directly what behavior they need to stop or action they need to take, as I did with the dangerous temperature spikes in my reptile cages.

For instance:

"You are not allowed to frighten my kids."

"Stop opening the kitchen cabinet doors."

"No more locking the door when I step outside to get the mail. That needs to stop."

You can also leave typed or written notes communicating directives to your ghost, placed in prominent places like the dining room table, or taped to a door. I did that when I wanted the ghosts in my house to attend a Zoom session I had with Morgan.

If you want them out of your house entirely, tell them "This is my home now. You need to leave. You are not welcome here. You need to go now." or words to that effect.

Tell them they can go into the light at the nearest funeral home when there's a wake or funeral and see all of their loved ones on the other side, including their beloved pets (that might entice them). But wherever they go, it cannot be your home. They need to leave now.

If you want to make the departure easier for them, you can provide the address of the nearest funeral home and leave it on the table for the ghost to see.

Then stop giving them any attention.

If they continue turning on lights, making noise, etc., ignore them. Spirits thrive on your notice and emotion. Don't give it to them. Act as if they have already left—and they'll probably tire of expending all that energy to haunt you to no avail, and head elsewhere.

Demons vs. Ghosts

Most of the activity people experience in their homes is caused by human earthbound spirits. Nonhuman spirits do not tend to bother people unless they are invited in or attracted by dark situations. Negative entities that were never human are usually called "demons." These may include evil spirits, devils, or fiends.

Obviously, these spirits are more dangerous than a human earthbound spirit. They are not to be taken lightly.

Fortunately, you are unlikely to ever have to deal with a demon, unless you participate in activities that attract them, or move into a place that was already inhabited by a demon due to the actions of previous occupants.

So what may attract demons?

- Practicing black magic intended to cause harm to others.
- Using a Ouija board. It opens the door wide to the spirit world, and if you're unlucky, a demon may saunter in.
- Deliberately summoning a demon. Some people do this as a lark, not believing it will work. Others do it as part of a black magic rite. Either way, it's a very, very bad idea.
- Violence such as domestic abuse or child abuse.
- Serious drug or alcohol addictions.
- Extreme negative emotions such as overwhelming fury, hatred, terror, and suicidal depression may attract the attention of a demon. These may be side effects of violence, contentious breakups, addictions, etc.
- Spending a lot of time focusing on demons or devils may also catch their attention. Some people avoid reading books about demons or watching videos or movies about them for this very reason.

Demons will not usually invade your home just because you are involved in any of the situations mentioned above. However, you can minimize your risk by avoiding them.

How can you tell if you may have a demon instead of a mere ghost in your home? Watch for these signs.

- Harsh, strange, growling that sounds unlike any animal you've ever heard.
- Unseen voices that threaten you or say horrible things.
- Loud banging on the walls, especially three knocks in a row, supposedly a demonic mockery of the Holy Trinity.
- Terrified dogs or cats. Even worse, pets may be found injured or (rarely) killed.
- Red eyes staring at you from the darkness.
- Bite marks, wounds, scratches, or claw marks that appear inexplicably—especially in threes (another mockery of the Trinity).
- Horrific, rotten smells like that of a dead body, rotten eggs (sulfur), spoiled meat, feces, or putrid decay.
- Crucifixes or religious items knocked off the wall. Mistreatment or disappearance of bibles, rosaries, or religious artifacts.
- A lot of seriously bad luck: frequent accidents, financial upsets, health problems, pets dying, etc. (Of course, a string of bad luck is not necessarily due to demons. If none of the other signs are present, it's probably not demonic in nature. It could be that someone has wished you ill and sent a curse or negativity your way—or it could just be random misfortune.)

The above signs can be part of demonic "infestation and

oppression" in which the demon tries to wear down the people in the home prior to actual possession. Exorcists outline the five steps to possession as "invitation, obsession, infestation, oppression and possession."

If you are experiencing signs like those mentioned above, do not try to deal with the situation on your own. Get professional help. Call the local Catholic diocese, your church, or religious leaders and tell them what is going on. Let them know you would like someone to come out to bless your home and everyone in it—and clear out any demonic presence.

Do this before the activity escalates to genuine possession.

If anyone in your home is experiencing symptoms such as those listed below, it may not just be your house that is infested. They may be possessed, and you may need an exorcist.

Signs of possession:

- Abnormal contortions of face or body.
- Superhuman strength (a frail old lady may toss a big man across a room, for instance).
- Speaking in languages they don't know.
- Spewing blasphemies and hurling horrific insults.
- Wounds that appear and disappear quickly.
- Growling like a violent animal.
- Acting very out of character, often with cruelty and/or violence, trying to frighten, threaten, or harm loved ones or others.
- Paranormal capabilities, such as floating in air or moving objects without touching them.
- Knowing things they can't possibly know (often private and disturbing things).
- Hatred for holy objects, church, prayers, holy water, and anything related to God.

A single exorcism may not be enough to get rid of a demon if it has become entrenched, but with persistence, it can be expelled.

Never give up!

LOVED ONES IN THE LIGHT

*"I shall not commit the fashionable stupidity
of regarding everything I cannot explain as a fraud."*
—C.G. Jung

Ghosts are spirits who have stuck around on the earth instead of going into the light. But most of our relatives and friends have gone into the light which leads to the afterlife. They can still come back from the other side and visit us—and they are always keeping track of what's happening in our lives, because they love us.

If you want to talk to loved ones who have gone into the light, it's easy. Just speak to them out loud and they will hear you.

The problem is, you may not hear their response. That's where dreams, mediums, or meditation can help. (And sometimes Alexa, who answered "You're welcome!" after I thanked all of my grandparents aloud for the love they showed me while alive. ☺)

Dreams

Our loved ones who have passed can show up as part of ordinary, nonsensical dreams. But sometimes we may have extremely vivid dreams that seem real, as if our loved one has genuinely come to visit and speak with us. These "visitations" feel different than ordinary dreams. They may wake you. They can remain memorable and vivid even years later.

You can communicate with your loved ones in these kinds of dreams and be confident that the conversation is real.

Some people complain that they never remember their dreams—or that their loved ones never appear in them. There are things you can do to remedy this.

- When you are about to go to sleep at night, ask specific loved ones to come to you in your dreams that night. You can also ask them to wake you right after they show up so that you can remember the dream. (We remember dreams better when we wake in the midst of them, during REM sleep.)
- Say aloud, "I will remember my dreams tonight." Set that intention and believe it.
- Place a bag or sachet with dried mugwort inside your pillowcase or underneath your pillow. In addition to mugwort, my dream bag includes dried rosemary, lavender and marigold flowers from my garden, as well as a small tumbled prehnite stone. Inhale the scent as you lie down to sleep.
- Place a piece of amethyst under your pillow to help you remember your dreams. Many people also use amethyst to help them sleep better.
- Pink amethyst and apatite are other stones recommended for helping you recall your dreams. You can place one under your pillow or on a bedside table.
- Make a tea or tincture of mugwort, spearmint, or peppermint and drink it before bedtime. This is reputed to help you have more vivid, lucid dreams.

- As soon as you wake up in the night or in the morning, try to remember your most recent dream without moving or changing position in bed. If your alarm is sounding, quickly turn it off with minimal movement. Do not listen to the news or music—which will rapidly destroy your memory of the dream. Try to trace the dream further back in your memory than the final moments.
- Describe your dream memory on your phone's voice recorder or write it down as soon as possible. I typically write a few notes on a little pad to retain the memory and then type up the full dream(s) with lots of details on the computer when I go downstairs. I usually edit the wording and add things as I go; the act of writing can boost recall.

Ever since I have been placing my dream bag and amethyst under my pillow, I have been able to remember my dreams with greater frequency. I think adding mugwort to my tea regimen—and writing down my dreams—have also boosted my dream recall. While this has led to some rather amazing dreams with spiritual themes (that I truly appreciate) unfortunately, it has not yielded new "visitation" dreams for me so far.

Mediums

Are mediums really connecting us with loved ones on the other side, or are they clever shysters and frauds? Based on my experience, I believe that some people genuinely do have the ability to speak to those in spirit form.

Unfortunately, there are many more people who take advantage of those grieving, and pretend to bring through information by using "cold reading" or "hot reading" techniques to get "hits." Although these fakes may make people feel better by bringing through supposed messages of love from the other side, their motivation is actually self-serving: to make money off fooling others.

People love watching psychic mediums perform on television, which explains the popularity of shows that have featured John Edward, James Van Praagh, Theresa Caputo, Chip Coffey, Tyler Henry, Kim Russo, Monica the Medium, John Holland, Thomas John and Allison DuBois.

Sadly, it has been reported that mistakes or "misses" may be edited out of the final footage so that a TV show will present a higher percentage of accurate information being brought through than actually occurred. This can be misleading.

False messages can even be dangerous, as in the infamous case in which a popular psychic wrongly claimed that a missing girl was dead. The mother ended up dying of heart failure a year later—and never learned her daughter was still alive when the girl finally escaped her captors.

Does that mean you should never see a psychic medium? If you don't believe in them, obviously don't go to one. Also, avoid phone and online "psychics" who advertise everywhere and charge by the minute. You are probably more psychic than they are.

However, I do believe there are people who have a genuine ability to reach across the veil. They could help you speak with your loved ones and bring you comfort and closure.

If you want to meet with a medium, don't just pick one randomly from an online listing. Only go to a medium that other people recommend—the more the better—ideally people you know. Ask them questions about their experience. What about the medium impressed them? How specific was the information? Did the medium bring through details they couldn't have found by doing a little research, such as unique memories that only you and your loved one shared? Did they know things that no one else but you and your loved one would know? Ask for specific examples.

This is called "evidential mediumship" and it's the only kind you should seek. Some mediums say generic things such as "I'm getting a grandmother figure. She liked to bake." This could fit more than half the grandmothers in the world! That's not genuine evidence. It sounds more like a guess than a real connection.

If a medium actually connects to your grandmother, they need to bring forth more specific information, such as a unique recipe that she made, or something unusual she said to you, or an unexpected gift she gave you—none of which you have written about on social media. Any information that's already out there will be used by unethical "mediums" to convince you they are legitimate.

Also, a genuine, ethical medium will never give you cruel or negative information. If the spirit says something harsh to them, they will find a kinder way to express it to you. (Fortunately, people on the other side do seem to mellow out a bit most of the time, so grumpy people who have died aren't as likely to say nasty things to us as when they were alive.)

If all of this makes you feel uncomfortable about trying to find a genuine medium, but you really want to talk to your loved ones on the other side, there is another option.

Be your own medium.

Communicating Directly

It takes two to communicate, one who is living on Earth and one who has gone on to the other side. Either one can initiate communication. It is then up to the other to respond.

Even if you aren't directly trying to instigate communication with loved ones who have passed, they may try to contact you. Below are some of the ways that spirits have reached out to loved ones on this side of the veil.

Pay attention. Your loved ones may use these methods in an effort to contact you.

How loved ones may reach out to you:

Feeling their presence

Just as we often know when someone is staring at us and look around to find their eyes upon us, we can sometimes sense that our loved one is nearby—even though we can't see them.

Hearing their voice

It's rare to hear the voice of a deceased loved one with your ears; it's more common to hear them speak to you telepathically (in your mind).

Touched by love

You could feel the touch of a loved one's hand on your body, stroking, tapping or holding you in an embrace, to let you know they are present, and that they love you.

Full apparition

You may see your loved one looking lifelike and completely solid—but healed and whole, no matter how they died. They may appear younger than when they passed. Whether they speak or not, their loving smile makes the message clear: they are fine and they love you.

Partial apparition

This may be easier for spirits to present to you than a full apparition. It can include just part of the body, such as the head and shoulders, their silhouette, or a figure of light. They may look transparent or almost completely solid.

Transitionary encounter

When you are very relaxed and between states of consciousness (with brainwaves in the alpha state), such as when meditating or in deep prayer, or transitioning into or out of sleep, you may see your loved one when you open your eyes.

"Visitation" dreams

Your loved one can come to you more easily when your brain is calm and quiet, not filled with tumbling thoughts. That's why many people have experienced encounters with deceased loved ones when asleep. These "visitations" are much more vivid than ordinary dreams. You will be able to have a conversation with your loved one and actually feel like they are really present—because they are.

I had one of these dreams after my Dad passed and it remains vivid to this day. It felt very different than my usual, crazy, mixed-up dreams.

Spirit to spirit

When you are asleep or in deep meditation, you may actually feel that your spirit has left your body and gone to a beautiful physical or spiritual location—where you feel filled with love and joy, and receive a visit from your loved one.

Phone from beyond

You may hear a phone ringing, and when you answer it, your loved one speaks. The voice may be clear but sound far away. Sometimes people have two-way conversations. When the call ends, there will be no sound of disconnection or a dial tone. This may happen when you are awake or asleep. Messages may also be left on computers or voicemail.

Also, I know of many people who have received a phone call from a deceased person's phone and when they answered it, there was silence on the other end. It's possible they couldn't hear the message their loved one was trying to convey, or the phantom call was simply a sign from their loved one that they are still connected with us from the other side.

Physical signs

Many people receive physical signs from loved ones, such as lights, TVs, toys, electronics of all kinds, turning off or on. You may see pictures or other objects moved or knocked over. Doors may open or close. I found a quarter in an impossible place that my Dad had put there.

Heavenly manifestations

Your loved one may send signs such as rainbows, specific birds, animals, flowers, butterflies, coins, feathers or pictures, especially if they represent your loved one in some way (such as a bird they loved or a coin with the date they died). Because these signs can be subtle, people may attribute them to mere coincidence. However, you will feel the difference intuitively.

For instance, once a butterfly kept landing on me and flying around me when I was outside in front of my house, working in my garden. It wouldn't leave; I had never experienced anything like that before (or since). I felt it was a sign. When I acknowledged the sign from my loved one aloud and expressed gratitude for it, the butterfly finally flew away.

How you may reach out to loved ones

Of course, you don't have to wait around for your loved ones to contact you from the other side; you can make an effort to contact them when you feel ready.

Many mediums suggest that you wait until your grief has abated a bit, because strong emotion can interfere with making a connection. Also, your loved one may need a little time on the other side to get adjusted and learn the best way of connecting with you across the veil. When you feel the time is right, try one or more of these methods:

Talk to them

You used to talk to your loved ones when they were alive, and you still can. Picture them in your mind or look at a photograph of them and start talking to them out loud (ideally in a quiet and private location so people won't get the wrong idea). Some people suggest that you ask your loved one a "yes" or "no" question and request that they respond by making a knocking sound or turning a light off or on. However, I think it can be hard for many spirits to manifest physical signs like that. I prefer to quiet my mind and listen for whatever they may telepathically want to tell me—because that's how spirits communicate, via telepathy (they have no vocal cords, after all). Although people often use recorders to ask questions of earthbound spirits and get EVP responses, I have not heard that spirits can still do this once they have gone into the light.

Write to them

You can write to your loved ones on a notepad or a key-board. I type my questions in a Word document on the comput-er because I can type much faster than I can write by hand—and then I type in whatever instantly comes to me, which I feel is their answer. Their responses and advice always seem wiser than I would come up with on my own. A nice thing about typing the conversation is that you have a concrete record of it that you can go back to again and again.

Meditate

Find a quiet place where you can sit or lie down without being disturbed. Try to clear your mind. If it helps, you can stare at a candle or repeat a word or phrase whenever thoughts start to intrude. Don't beat yourself up if your mind starts to wander. Simply go back to emptying your mind. Many people start by meditating for just five or 10 minutes. This helps to reduce stress and when done regularly, can open you up to the spirit world over time. When you feel ready to communicate with your loved one, clear your mind and focus on their face for as long as you can. Listen for what pops into your mind (without trying to think it up).

Hold a prized possession

To boost a connection with your loved one, you can hold a belonging that they loved while they were on Earth, or an article of their clothing. Feel their energy present in the object. Mediums often hold objects to read information through psychometry—but in this case, you already know who owned the object and are simply trying to tune into their vibe. Combine this with meditation by focusing on the object as you clear your mind, or talk to them aloud while holding the object.

Ask for signs

Ask your loved one to send you a sign that they are with you—or to answer a question that you have asked. You can ask to see a rainbow, a specific bird, animal or flower, butterflies, coins, feathers or a photograph of some place or thing that was special to your loved one. You may receive the signs as the physical thing itself or they may appear unexpectedly as a picture, video, or words on a website, or in an email or letter that you receive. Trust your intuitive feeling that the sign was from your loved one.

Dare to dream

Although loved ones may appear in your dreams unbidden, you can also ask that they come to you in that way. Because your mind is more open when you sleep, it may be easier for them to reach you then. Ask them to appear in your dreams when you lie down to sleep. Tell yourself "I will remember my dream with {Name} tonight." You can also try to take control of a dream. As soon as you awaken from one, close your eyes and imagine yourself back in the dream; let yourself drift back into it knowing you are dreaming.

Patience and gratitude

You may not make contact with your loved one immediately—or you may get responses or signs that are so subtle, you don't trust them. Don't be disheartened—and don't give up. Try different methods at different times, always when you're calm and in a quiet place, not emotionally overwhelmed or distracted.

Your loved one may be busy on the other side, or still trying to figure out how to respond to you. It's not easy for them to converse with us through the veil. Keep your eyes, intuition, and mind open, and your loved one will eventually be able to get through.

When you do get a response, remember to thank your loved one. Your gratitude will encourage them to make the effort to reach out to you again. But don't expect them to be in constant communication. They have other things to do!

ANGELS ACT

"Angels can fly because they take themselves lightly"
—*G.K. Chesterton*

I was raised to believe that we each have a guardian angel that stays with us throughout our entire life. It was just a belief until I started to have a real relationship with my angel. Now I have no doubt.

Your guardian angel is always ready to help you. But you need to ask for their assistance. We all have free will and they don't want to overstep their bounds.

One cold winter day, I was driving over a bridge. The car in front of me braked suddenly, nearly stopping in the middle of the freeway. I put my foot on the brake pedal, but my car kept sliding forward, not slowing at all. I had apparently hit a large patch of black ice.

As I tried again to apply my brakes, my vehicle started fishtailing and I was afraid I would hit the railing on the side of the bridge. Inches away from crashing into the car in front of me, I cried out to my guardian angel: "Help me!

To this day, I cannot explain what happened. The distance between our vehicles instantly increased from mere inches to

142

several feet, and I did not see that expansion take place. I was saved from a car accident that seemed inevitable.

It was like space/time had been momentarily transformed. It boggled my mind.

Dee told me when she was a young girl, she was in a hurry to get to a nearby skating rink on a lake near her home. She was so excited to try out her new skates, she didn't stop to look both ways before crossing the street.

As she stepped onto the pavement, she felt a hand forcefully grab her by the shoulder and yank her backward. She looked around to see who was responsible, but no one was there.

At the same moment, a car roared around the corner, speeding down the street right where Dee had been about to step. If an unseen guardian hadn't pulled Dee back, the vehicle would have hit her.

In rare instances, angels will intervene like this—unasked—to save a life when it's not that person's time to move on to the afterlife. But for the most part, angels need us to ask for their help. (I'm sure sometimes they're dying for us to ask so they can rush to our aid.)

That doesn't mean your guardian angel is a servant who will do whatever you request and give you everything you want. They cannot do something that is not in your best interest spiritually—like giving you winning lottery numbers. They are much more concerned with helping your soul than fulfilling your material desires.

It can be difficult when we ask our angels to heal someone, and it doesn't happen. But I believe it is part of our journey on Earth to deal with challenges and heartbreak—which help us to grow much more than living through easy times. Suffering can make us more compassionate toward others, and also help us to become more focused on spirituality, as long as we avoid falling into the pitfalls of anger, bitterness, or cynicism.

Always remember that death is not the worst thing that can happen to someone. Those who have died feel no pain—and get to move on to something better. It is only we who suffer as we mourn the loss of their physical presence.

If your guardian angel cannot extend the life of a loved one, they can certainly help you deal with your grief over that loss. Reach out to them. Ask them difficult questions and listen for their wise and loving answers.

When I lost a dear friend, I was worried I would break down at the funeral service. I asked my guardian angel, "How can I keep my composure during the funeral?"

He replied, "Think on God, not Nellie. God is with you. Feel that. Peace is Nellie's—and yours, if you trust in God. Trust that God knows what S/He is doing in taking Nellie.

Also, you will see Nellie again. This is not a final goodbye, just a temporary one. Nellie is much happier now."

I felt peace envelop me as my guardian angel spoke. That brief conversation helped me get through the funeral.

Angel Prayers

I was taught a prayer to my guardian angel when I was a small child, and sometimes I still say it. There are also prayers and invocations for seeking help from the archangels.

Traditional Guardian Angel Prayer

Angel of God, my guardian dear,
God's love for me has sent you here.
Ever this day be at my side,
To light and guard, to rule and guide.

Evening Angel Prayer

> Angels bless and angels keep,
> Angels guard me while I sleep.
> Bless my heart and bless my home.
> Bless my spirit as I roam.
> Guide and guard me through the night
> and wake me with the morning light.
> Amen.

Traditional Prayer to St. Michael

Saint Michael the Archangel, defend us in battle. Be our safeguard against the wiles and wickedness of the devil. Restrain him, O God, we humbly pray, and do thou, O Prince of the heavenly Host, by the power of God, cast into Hell Satan and all the evil spirits, who prowl about the world seeking the ruin and destruction of souls. Amen.

Morning Prayer to St. Michael

> Michael, Michael of the morning,
> Fresh chord of Heaven adorning,
> Keep me safe today,
> And in time of temptation
> Drive the devil away.
> Amen.

There are also specific prayers to St. Michael reserved for use during an exorcism, since he is known to have great power over devils and demons. These prayers are used by priests, not the general public.

If you want to spend more time with Michael the Archangel—and all of the angels—you can say a Chaplet Prayer on a string of beads (a bit like a rosary) that includes nine salutations that correspond to the nine Choirs of Angels, and also honors Gabriel, Raphael and your own Guardian Angel. There is something very satisfying about praying in such a tactile way, sliding the beads through your fingers as you move through the Chaplet.

Most sources recognize three or four archangels by name: Michael, Gabriel, Raphael, and often, Uriel. These are mentioned in various religious texts. The first three are celebrated in the Catholic Church on their feast day of September 29th.

Additional archangel names can be found in apocryphal sources; there is no consensus on the names, although some are cited in multiple texts, lending them more credence. Many of these names have been popularized over the years, such as Jophiel, Chamuel, Zadkiel, Raguel, Azrael, Haniel, and Raziel. You'll notice that all of these names end in "el". That's because the suffix "el" means "of God" or "God", indicating who the angels serve.

Here is a way in which you can call on the power of the four most recognized archangels to protect you throughout the day.

Archangel Guards

Ask these four archangels to stand around you, and go with you throughout your day, protecting and guiding you.

Michael on the right (he stands for Protection)
Uriel on the left (he stands for Wisdom)
Raphael in front (he stands for Healing)
Gabriel in back (he stands for Communication)

Remember to thank them for their assistance.

The Name of Your Guardian Angel

If you want to know your guardian angel's name, ask them about it while doing the visualization technique described in the next section. Be open to whatever comes to you.

Many people think that angels have a unique language that we cannot understand. If so, their name in that language might be unintelligible to us. In that case, they may provide a name in our language that has a similar meaning or that they think we will like.

You can also suggest a name to them. Whatever makes you comfortable is perfect. I don't think your guardian angel cares what you call them as long as you have a relationship with them.

I like the traditional angel names that end in "el" meaning "of God" so when I asked my guardian angel for his name, I got one that ended in "el" too. It reflects my need to be courageous and open to new things. "Dariel" encourages me to *dare* to expand my dreams, my vision, and my heart while on my path to the Divine.

Ideally, your angel name will have a special significance or personal appeal to you.

ANGEL HEART-TO-HEARTS

"Make yourself familiar with the angels,
and behold them frequently in spirit;
for without being seen, they are present with you."
—Saint Francis de Sales

I have to admit that I rarely recite rote prayers because they feel confining and a bit stilted to me. I would rather have a conversation with my guardian angel or the archangels directly, speaking in my own words about my specific concerns.

You can speak aloud or talk to them telepathically; since they are spirits, they can "hear" either form of communication. However, I feel the interaction is much richer if I can also "see" my angel companion as we are conversing.

This just requires a little visualization.

Find a comfortable place where you won't be disturbed. Sit or lie down, get comfortable, and close your eyes. Picture a beautiful place where you would love to be.

I often see a gorgeous flower garden with a bluff behind it, a pristine lake in front, mountains in the distance, and a forest on each side. There is an ornate but comfortable bench set up right against the bluff, facing the flower garden, the lake. and the mountains. I sit there looking at the beautiful scenery, calming my mind, breathing slowly and deeply. Then my guardian angel joins me on the bench. We have a conversation. Often I'm amazed by the wisdom and love that my angel offers me. After our conversation is finished (I usually know when I've gotten what I need), I will often write down what transpired so I don't forget it.

There are other locations where I meet my angel as well. Sometimes I step through a circle of light, like a door to another realm, and there's a lovely little stone cottage with a thatched roof on the edge of a woods. It sits on a low cliff in front of an ocean. The top of the door is rounded, and the windows are circular, too.

I unlock the cottage with a skeleton key and sit on an antique velvet sofa in front of a bright, crackling fire in the hearth. I breathe slowly and start to relax. Soon my angel joins me, and we converse here as we do by the flower garden. Again, I write down our conversation afterwards.

I will go back and reread the most luminous sessions, because I need to be reminded of the sage advice I was given in order to stay on track. I seem to keep making the same mistakes. (As I keep saying to Dariel, "I'm sorry I'm such a slow learner!" He has encouraged me by saying I AM learning, so it's okay.)

Where would you like to meet your angel? Is there a place that you particularly love or where you feel most comfortable? Is there a dream landscape where you would love to spend time?

I created meeting locations that appeal to me, but you may prefer to meet on a sandy beach or on a mountaintop, in a beautiful church, or on a boat; choose any place that resonates with you and lifts your heart.

When I'm out and about during the day and don't have the time for a detailed meditation, I simply visualize my guardian angel standing behind me with his hands on my shoulders. I feel him there and I know he's got my back. I talk to him telepathically and listen for his guidance. The more you communicate with your angel, the easier it becomes.

It can be very helpful to take a moment to talk to your guardian angel while at work, without a full-blown visualization.

One day, I was feeling very overwhelmed by all the things on my plate. I didn't see how I could get everything done and I was tired of working long hours. I felt very down. I took a moment to talk to Dariel.

Me: "Dariel, what is wrong with me? Why am I so sad?"

Dariel: "You need time for yourself. It's that simple."

Me: "How can I get it?"

Dariel: "Make it. Right now. And stop worrying. Worry about *nothing*. Only deal with problems as they arise."

Me: "Should I take a walk?"

Dariel: "Yes. And talk to me."

I let everything go and took a walk outside, speaking telepathically with Dariel as I went. It helped to get away from the building, and to circle a nearby pond where geese swam.

It didn't take long, so I didn't guilt myself over taking the short break. I definitely felt better after that. I was able to re-enter my day with a more positive mindset, which benefited both me and my coworkers.

Another day at the office, I was trying to figure out what to do about a coworker who was often rude to me. I couldn't tell if she disliked me, was jealous of me, or was just taking out her frustrations on me because I happened to be there. I wondered if I should invite her on an outing. I wasn't sure if it was a good idea or not. So I talked to my guardian angel about it.

Me: "Dariel, what should I do about Saturday? Should I invite Shirley?"

Dariel: "Would it be seen as a peace offering?"

Me: "Maybe."

Dariel: "What's the advantage of that?"

Me: "She may feel more conciliatory toward me. I feel like there's tension between us right now. But it might feel awkward if I ask her to go."

Dariel: "If she thinks so, she may simply decline."

Me: "True, but at least I'll have extended the olive branch. I'll do it. Thanks, Dariel. I love you."

Dariel: "And I, you."

Oftentimes, simply discussing things with my guardian angel helps me to see it from a different perspective. He will ask me questions that help me come to a decision.

He clearly doesn't want to tell me what to do; he knows I need to freely make my own choices, good or bad.

Here's another example of how a conversation with Dariel helped me make a decision. I had run across a large wooden carving (about 30" x 19") on eBay featuring the scene of an angel talking to a man whose eyes were closed. It was clearly quite old, had cracks and stains, and one of the man's arms was missing. Antiques Roadshow had appraised the artwork as being from the 1600s, and stated that it had likely originated in Germany. The seller had documentation of its provenance which proved that it had been brought to America by a wonderful artist many years earlier.

I loved the look of the piece, and its age. I wasn't sure I should bid on it, though. The opening bid alone was expensive, although I thought that cost was very reasonable, compared to similar pieces I had seen. Also, the seller said the artwork was too fragile to ship. She would only allow a buyer to come to her home and pick it up. The seller lived about 1,000 miles away from me—which would require a very long car trip—and I couldn't afford to take the time off from work.

Lots of people from all over the country were interested in buying the angel artwork, but the seller's unwillingness to ship it was stymieing their bids. Then the seller informed me that she had a friend who just happened to be driving up to visit relatives close to where I lived, and she could deliver the carving to me. It seemed like a godsend, but should I spend the money? I stewed about it for a while before finally deciding to discuss it with Dariel.

Me: "Dear Dariel, I am torn. Should I bid on the angel carving or not?"

Dariel: "What do you think?"

Me: "On the one hand, I'm attracted to it. It's beautiful and old, and would make a fabulous focal point in our living room. I love the subject matter and its history. It actually has a documented provenance. On the other hand, it's in rough shape. Would people think I was crazy for buying it? Is it selfish of me to spend that much money on something I don't need when there are people starving?"

Dariel: "Can you save all of the starving?"

Me: "No, but I could send that money to them."

Dariel: "You do send money to the poor now."

Me: "Probably not enough. I'm spending a lot on my kids' college costs right now. And we need to do some upkeep on the house. Would I regret buying the piece? That's my biggest concern. Would I find it less impressive in person than in the pictures? Would it be hard for the kids to sell some day when I'm gone? Why do I want it?"

Dariel: "Why do you want it?"

Me: "The angel subject matter first brought it to my attention—and its age. Those are both things I love. I also wonder if this is my only opportunity to afford a piece like this. Because it's not in perfect condition, it's less costly than a similar, perfect piece—which would probably cost thousands—more than I could pay. Similarly aged but less appealing pieces on eBay are listed for higher opening bids. Of course, someone could swoop in at the last minute and buy it for a higher bid. Help me decide!"

Dariel (LAUGHTER): "It's not as important as you're making it. If you don't buy it, you might regret it, and if you do, you might as well. You tend to overthink some things, and not think enough about others."

Me: "Like what?"

Darel: "Think about it."

Me: "I want to do the right thing."

Darel: "So you say."

Me: "What does God want me to do?"

Dariel: "Listen to your inner voice."

Me: "Is He saying not to spend the money? Why is the seller's name, Victoria, then? (That's my daughter's name.) Why did she come up with a way to get it to me for free, then? Are these just added temptations I'm supposed to overcome?"

Dariel: Laughs.

Me: "You're not helping."

Dariel: "Listen to your inner voice."

Me: "Why didn't you send me a dream?"

Dariel: "I did."

Me: "What?"

Dariel: "I sent you an angel."

His last comment hit me like a shock. I instantly knew he had actually sent this opportunity to me. He knew that I would truly love and appreciate the angel artwork. No other interested buyer had received my wonderful synchronicity: that a friend of the seller's was just happening to be driving up near where I lived, so the artwork could be delivered from a thousand miles away.

I ended up getting the piece for the minimum bid. We secured it to the wall above our mantel, where it stays to this day. Every time I look at it, I still love it. And I am grateful for Dariel's wisdom and the circumstances that brought it to me.

Write To Your Angel

Just as you can write to your deceased loved ones in spirit, you can write to your guardian angel, either on paper or electronically. I type my questions or concerns on the computer—and then type the response that flows from Dariel.

Note that if the response is truly from an angel, it will be kind, wise, and encouraging. Your angel will never say anything negative to you, or direct you to do anything not in keeping with the light. If you get a negative response, it is probably your skeptical or self-doubting subconscious mind that is sabotaging you. Stop typing and take some time to breathe deeply and slowly until you feel relaxed. If you feel up to it, try again—or wait for another time.

ASK FOR AN ANGEL SIGN

*"Whatever you put your attention on in this life
will increase in your life. As you put your attention on angels,
they will begin increasingly to make their presence known to
you."*
—Denise Linn

If you want to connect in a very concrete way, you can ask your angel for a sign. I typically ask for a feather as I am walking outdoors. To me, this is simply a sign that my angel is with me and has my back.

Once I found a gorgeous fluffy white feather on an icy deserted sidewalk in the middle of winter. The feather looked perfect, like it had just fallen from the sky. It did not look like a feather that would have been part of a coat or any form of clothing. I had not seen any birds around that had feathers like this in January (in Minnesota) either. It was very encouraging at a dark moment in my life.

Sometimes, I have even seen unexpected feathers on my path indoors. I always chalk this up to angel encouragement.

Another sign Dariel will often send me is a heart-shaped stone. I'll be out walking along a road and suddenly, right in front of me, will be a rock with that tell-tale shape. I always pick up these stones and bring them home, because they make me smile every time I see them. I have amassed a small collection of these signs of the love and presence of my guardian angel.

Dariel also says hello to me and reminds me that he is here for me via the number "11". Whenever I chance to look at a clock and it reads 8:11, 10:11, 7:11, 11:11—basically whenever it is 11 minutes past the hour—I always say hi to my angel and have a moment with him. I don't actively seek that specific time. It happens by chance and not by my waiting around for that time to occur.

When I see "11" in other contexts that seem significant, my angel may have a message for me at that moment. For example, being assigned to Concourse 11 at an airport may mean that my angel is protecting me on my flight, or that I will have a successful trip.

Many people see "444" as a sign from their angel. Let your angel know if there is a number that has a special meaning for you, so they can use it to send you messages.

Also ask your angel for specific signs that have personal significance to you.

Angel Dreams

Angels can visit you in your dreams just as deceased loved ones can. In the Bible, Joseph repeatedly received important messages in dreams. Even today, they may give life-saving messages in this way.

People have dreamed angels told them they were seriously ill, or that they might die if they didn't take certain actions. When one woman visited a doctor after her dream, and had some medical tests, she learned she had an aggressive form of cancer—which was caught early enough to be cured. When others dreamt they should cancel a flight—and followed that directive—they later learned the plane had crashed.

I have not had such dramatic life-saving angel dreams, but I did have a dream about my spiritual path featuring Dariel that clarified something important to me. More vivid than a normal dream, it sticks with me, still. (Please forgive me for not sharing it; it was very personal.)

If you do get a message from an angel in your dreams, let your intuition help you judge how you should respond. You can also ask your angel for more guidance, if needed.

Of course, not every dream that includes angels is a sign or a message from Heaven. Our subconscious uses all kinds of images to create wacky dreams that may just happen to include an angel. Look at how the angels appear in your dream and consider what they say. If they act ridiculous or say nasty things, they are not genuine angels, but simply your subconscious acting up.

Gratitude Is Your Gift

Angels can give us great advice, guidance, love, and support. They can even save our lives. But what can we give them in return?

Gratitude! Tell them frequently how thankful you are for their help, and for their presence in your life. Everyone loves to be appreciated, and angels are no exception.

Yes, it's their job to help us on our path. But it's our job to follow the path of love, which includes expressing gratitude—a blessing to others.

ANGELS VS. HUMANS

*"One thing is clear: Angels are far more than projections
of the divine mind or literary devices.
They are real, personal beings,
even if their corporeality is totally different from ours."*
—*Eileen Elias Freeman*

I had some concerns and questions that I brought to God in conversation one day about the nature of angels and human beings. I was told that people have more layers than angels. We change and grow because we were created to do so.

Angels are more static in nature. They are steadfast in their character, always in spirit form (except for brief forays into our world when they have a special mission), and they are always directly connected to God.

All living things (animals, people, plants) on Earth were created to transform and evolve. It's a core characteristic—and something that makes us particularly interesting. We never stay the same—because we aren't meant to!

Some people try to keep things from changing because they feel insecure when the world transforms. They may think things are "going to hell" when society changes from what it was like when they grew up. In every age, for hundreds and probably thousands of years, some people have thought that the young were ruining things because they were doing things differently. (It's funny to read ancient diatribes about this, and compare them to what people say today—that, at least, has not changed!)

But God wants us to grow. God gave us the gift of creativity to create NEW things, not to simply repeat the old over and over. God enjoys seeing us express our creativity and wants to see us evolve and become better—both individually and as a society.

God does not want us to stagnate and remain in a box, unchanging.

If that's scary to you, remember that you have a stalwart guardian angel always beside you, who is NOT changing in their guidance and their love for you. They are your rock in a world and a life filled with transformation.

Think of your life as the caterpillar and pupae stages of a butterfly. Your experiences in this world are like the weaving of your cocoon. God and your guardian angel are the solid tree to which you (and your cocoon) are attached. The tree will remain strong and steadfast as you transform inside your lifespan/cocoon. In the afterlife, you will emerge as the butterfly, wiser and better because of your experiences on Earth in a material body.

We are meant to feel a bit of separation from God in this life so that we can fully express our creativity and not be overwhelmed by the power of the Divine. However, having a connection with Spirit can help us to experience a happier and deeper life on Earth.

SPIRIT GUIDES

"Every human being has, like Socrates,
an attendant spirit; and wise are they who obey its signals."
—Lydia M. Child

When you pass onto the other side, what do you think you will be doing? Wouldn't it be boring to sit on a cloud strumming harps all day as comic strips have often depicted? Eternity is a long time.

We may want to learn new things from the wisest souls on the other side. We may want to take on a new challenge, in keeping with all that we have learned. We may eventually want to help guide others who are going through circumstances similar to what we endured on Earth, or who are struggling with problems that we were able to master. Wouldn't it feel good to be able to use your wisdom and skills to help someone else?

That is what spirit guides have chosen to do. They are not guardian angels, but souls who have been on earth, and want to help guide us from their vantage point in the light as we move through life. We can ask them for help, talk to them, and listen for their answers, much as we do with angels.

Catholics have been doing a similar thing with saints throughout the ages. They talk to saints and ask them for help and signs (such as the sign of roses that comes from St. Terese). These holy people could certainly be a part of your team of spirit guides. But the canonized aren't the only ones who have wisdom to share.

Your Spirit Guides

Years ago, I took a weekend workshop from two well-known psychic mediums who traveled to my town to teach attendees how to meet and connect with their spirit guides. It was eye-opening. They explained that each of us has one "master spirit guide" who will be with us from birth to death, just like our guardian angel.

Additional guides may come and go as we need them; they are often specialists who send signs and synchronicities ("wonderful coincidences" or "Godwinks") to help guide us through specific challenges such as starting a family, going through a divorce, dealing with disability, or finding a new job.

Your team of spirit guides will include your master guide, subject matter guides, and loved ones—both people and pets—who are now in spirit. Many people also believe that we have a "higher self", the eternal part of our soul that is still in spirit while we are on Earth, and that this is also part of our team of guides.

Your guides have been with you throughout your life, sending you signals whether you were aware of it or not. Thoughts that just pop into your head may actually be ideas and guidance that they have sent you. Especially if these "thoughts" are unusually wise, insightful, solve problems, give you hope, inspire you to create something new or transform your life. Negative, angry, fearful, insulting, or hate-filled thoughts do NOT come from your spirit guides, who operate from a place of love—always.

They are our best friends in Spirit.

* * *

Meeting Your Master Guide

To meet your master spirit guide for the first time, use a visualization technique, as you did when meeting with your guardian angel.

Find a comfortable place where you won't be disturbed. Sit or lie down, get comfortable, and close your eyes. Tell your master spirit guide aloud, or in your mind, of your intention to meet them. Invite them to come to you.

Take several slow, deep breaths, exhaling more slowly than you inhale, until you feel relaxed. Picture a glowing archway in the middle of a meadow. Walk through it. You instantly find yourself in another place.

There is a beautiful lake with a sandy beach in front of you, not too far away, and a luminous forest all around it. Light fog over the lake drifts in and out of the trees.

Walk to the shore and look into the still water. You see your reflection. Take several slow, deep breaths as you relax.

Eventually you see the reflection of someone else as they walk up behind you, smiling. Their love for you is so deep, you feel it. This is your master guide. What do they look like?

Turn around to greet them. If it feels right, embrace them. Let their love wash over you. You want to get to know this one, who has made you the center of their afterlife.

Since your master guide may have used many names over time, ask "What shall I call you?" instead of "What's your name?" Together, agree on the name that feels right.

Before you ever met your guide, they were subtly guiding you and keeping you safe, planting thoughts in your head and sending signs and synchronicities to keep you on track and make life better for you.

Isn't this a good time to thank them for all they have done for you?

Now that you have met them, they can help you even more—because you can ask for their assistance whenever you need or want it.

Sit down with your master spirit guide on a bench or a log near the lake and have a conversation. Ask them questions and listen to their answers. Be open to their insight on any decisions you need to make, or challenges you are dealing with.

Ask for a Sign

If you feel hesitant because you fear you're just imagining the whole thing, ask your guide to give you a sign—something you want them to make happen in the material world to confirm that they are indeed real—so you can believe in and trust them as your guide. Give them a time frame (such as two or three weeks—not a year) in which to show you the sign.

Set reasonable parameters for the sign; your guide needs to work with what's in our world. Don't ask for an alien spacecraft to land in your backyard. Also, don't ask for a million dollars to fall in your lap; your guide is here to help you grow spiritually, not to become ultra-rich.

Don't tell anyone else about the sign you're looking for—or you may doubt the results, suspecting the person you told made it happen, instead of your guide.

Also, don't get too literal in accepting the sign when you receive it. They're doing the best they can with what they have to work with. If you ask them to send a manatee to your house, you may get a magazine in the mail with a manatee on the front. Or your child may bring a manatee sticker home from school. Don't discount these as the signs you requested.

How I Met My Guide

163

I first met my master spirit guide during a visualization exercise at the weekend workshop I attended on spirit guides. When I met and spoke with her, my heart started pounding so hard! She felt like a sister from a previous life. Our connection was that close.

Her hair was long, straight, and silvery. She wore a light, ankle-length gown and sandals. Her attire reminded me of something women would have worn in ancient Greece.

A name for her popped into my head: "Silvina." It is not a name I had ever encountered in this world. Later I looked up the meaning of "Silvina" online and found that it means "woodland forest." I'm a "woods-and-water" loving person, so her name was perfect, especially since her silvery hair also matched the "Silv-" start to the name.

I was shocked and moved by the whole encounter. But of course, afterwards, I wondered if my imagination had simply made it all up.

According to the mediums teaching the workshop, my reaction was very normal. That's why we need to ask for a sign to validate what happened.

Owl or Fox?

I asked Silvina to send me a live owl or fox to prove that she was real and not just a figment of my imagination. I wanted to see one without going to a zoo or a raptor center. I wanted to see the sign in 2 weeks or less from the day I asked for it. That would be my validation.

Right after that, a video about owls showed up on my Facebook feed. It was charming, but I thought that it wasn't proof of Silvina. The owls were alive in the video, but I wasn't seeing them "live".

Then, on Instagram, I saw a cake that a friend had made for her one-year-old's birthday topped by marvelous little figures of a fox, an owl, and a bear. It had both of the animals that I had given Silvina as options to send me, but they weren't alive, so again I discounted this as a sign.

When my husband and I went on vacation to a B&B in Charleston, it was two days past the two-week time limit I had given Silvina, and I felt disappointed I had not seen a live fox or owl. Maybe she wasn't real after all.

The owner of the B&B was very welcoming and friendly, and wanted to show me her son's bedroom. We walked in—and there was a real stuffed gray fox, which looked very much alive. I have to admit, the taxidermy was pretty impressive. What were the odds that I would come to a B&B that had a fox, especially after I had specifically asked to see one?

I could picture Silvina tearing her pretty silver hair out, crying, "I've been trying so hard to give you validation, but you're not buying it." I almost started laughing. In my gut, I acknowledged that Silvina *had* fulfilled my validation request.

But I guess I'm a tough customer. I asked for another sign.

I told her I wanted to hear an owl hooting. And that summer, I heard one in the backyard of our house.

So eventually, I got both the owl AND the fox.

Ask For Guidance with Signs and Symbols

The time to ask your master spirit guide for signs and symbols isn't only when you want to validate their existence. You can also ask for signs when you want to validate a decision or a path.

Over the years, several different psychics have told me I was supposed to write a book.

I have co-authored a novel and written articles for magazines and newspapers, but I wasn't sure I was the right person to tackle these topics, even though I am passionate about them.

So I asked Silvina for some sign of the presence of an owl as I walked through a wooded area near my home—if indeed I was supposed to write a book on ghosts, guides, and guardians.

I have never seen or heard an owl there, to this day. But on that afternoon, I came across not one, but two owl pellets. (Owl pellets are similar to a cat's hairball—containing fur and bones that an owl cannot digest and therefore spits out.) One had within it a very tiny perfect skull—which I took home. Those pellets were certainly the sign of an owl's presence that I had asked for—although not in the form of hearing a hoot or seeing a bird perched in a tree, as I had expected.

It certainly appeared to confirm that I was meant to write this book. And it was a reminder that the signs we receive may not come in the form we anticipate; so, try to remain open and aware.

How You May Experience Your Guides

Although I have seen some of my guides in my mind's eye, some people never receive an image of their guides. They may hear messages in their mind, or get signs in the world that speak to them—like a song on the radio with an answer to their question, a particular bird that shows up, a butterfly that lands on their finger, or a coin that has the date they needed.

Be open to whatever happens, to however you personally connect with your guides. You are unique and your relationship with them is like no one else's. Feel it. Trust your gut, your intuition, when you get a sign.

Of course, the true test is whether the message you receive is loving and helpful. If it's not, it's your fearful ego talking, not your guides.

One morning, I complained to my spirit guides for the umpteenth time about being a slow learner.

Me: "I should be doing more!"

Spirit guides: "You should be "being" more. You are here to work on yourself—not anyone else. That is your primary goal in this life, to evolve your soul. Quit worrying about everyone else. If you can help others, do so. But your first focus needs to be on becoming the best version of yourself. Learn on your path.

"Don't try to change others. They're on their own path. Don't judge. Love. Love everyone. Love in spite of differences. If you loved yourself more, it would be easier to love others more, too."

It was clear they were suggesting that I needed to meditate more, to simply "be" more, to connect within. They asked me to ponder:

"How can you love yourself more?

How can you spread love and light?"

Clearly, our spirit guides can not only help us to navigate this life, they can also help us to grow. They want us to become more loving to ourselves and to others.

Evil actions come from people who are driven by fear. They have forgotten what we are all meant to express: Love and Light.

WAYS GUIDES CAN HELP YOU

Every morning you can ask your guides, "What do I need to know about today?" You can also say, "Please guide me every step of the way." Quiet your mind and listen for their insight.

You always have the option to use your free will to make a different choice than what you sense they are recommending. They will never interfere with your freedom—although they may be persistent in giving advice when they know it's for your own good. (If you get a persistent feeling that you need to see a dentist or a doctor for an issue, do it!)

Check in with your guides throughout the day. If you need to find an item or even a parking space in a crowded lot, ask for their help. They can tell you what to tackle next on your to-do list if you're not sure. They can help you say the right thing to an angry spouse or relative. They can direct you to a particular store—where you may find something you've been seeking, or run into an old friend you haven't seen in ages. They can help you choose a new house or the right school for your children. All you have to do is ask, quiet your mind, and be open to their advice.

You can also ask things like:

- How can I mend my relationship with _____?

- What do I need to let go of?
- How do I go about forgiving _____?
- How can I improve my relationship with my spouse/partner?
- What are my strengths and weaknesses as a parent?
- How can I get rid of the fears that are blocking me?
- What are my best qualities or talents, and how can I share them with the world?
- What is an important goal for me in this life?
- What do I need to do next?

Spend some time actively listening for their wise advice—then thank them for it!

At a time when the world seemed to be an utter disaster (Russia had attacked Ukraine; COVID was still spreading; climate change threatened the world; lies, riots and divisions were everywhere, etc.) I complained to my spirit guides about how hard things were.

They promptly replied, "This is an Advanced Lesson. Choose love, not fear."

How nice that they thought we were up to the challenge. But choosing to love murderous dictators is easier said than done!

A wise man recommended that I think of those who perform violent or hate-filled actions as the poorest of the poor. They are on the lowest level of humanity and need our help. We must not return their hatred with hate, but instead, do whatever we can to help them to transform and grow, such as sending prayers or wishes for them to do so.

My spirit guides have also told me, "This world is an adventure. Enjoy it! Pursue that which brings you joy. Don't be anxious or worried about anything. God is with us. No matter what happens, it will be right and fine in the end."

Your guides are committed to your growth and well-being. You, in turn, can commit to building a relationship with them. Talk to them daily and your communication will become clearer. Your trust and confidence will grow—and life will become easier.

In addition to sending you messages or insights, your spirit guides can make things happen for your benefit. Sudden synchronicities or serendipity in your life is often (maybe always) due to their actions on your behalf—the ideal job that you get because of a chance meeting, the perfect venue that suddenly opens up for your wedding, the world-renowned physician who just happens to be visiting your hospital when you need a complicated emergency operation.

I experienced a little serendipity as I was writing this. I had not yet found a quote to start off the "Spirit Guides" section of this book when I happened to read an entry from a daily meditations book I enjoy. That's when I saw a quote that led me to the one I chose to use about the attendant spirit of Socrates.

Always thank God and your spirit team—your guardian angel and your spirit guides—for their help in making these blessings happen, be they large or small. Gratitude brings additional grace into your life.

How Many Spirit Guides Do We Have?

We all have one main master spirit guide who is with us throughout our life, just as our guardian angel is. However, most mediums and psychics believe that we have additional spirit guides that come and go. As young children, we may not need much additional help, but as we grow and mature, facing more difficult challenges, additional guides arrive to assist us on our path.

These guides are specialists who have the expertise we need. When we first start dating, we may get quiet guidance from a spirit guide on love or relationships. A guide who is adept with money may help us when we are facing difficult decisions about investments or income. If we encounter troubles in our family, a family counselor guide may arrive. Guides for specific skills or careers may also help many people in their work lives.

Some people believe we have just one or two spirit guides as kids, but in the prime of our adulthood, we may have as many as a dozen. As we age and need less guidance, that number may go back down to just a couple.

You don't really need to know how many guides you have, or all their names. Simply ask your questions or tell them what you need, addressing your "spirit guide team."

I also sometimes ask for help from "Silvina and my other spirit guides," or request assistance from a particular spirit guide by name.

My Special Guide for This Book

I was able to write the first 38,000 words of this book fairly quickly because I had taken lots of notes about my and others' interactions with ghosts, fascinated by the new paranormal world that had opened up to me.

But when I started writing the "Guardians and Guides" sections, the territory was much more personal, dealing with internal versus external experiences, and I felt less secure about it.

Many of us have seen physical evidence of ghosts. A light turning on, an object flying across the room, a door opening by itself—these are all concrete signs suggesting a ghost may be present.

However, most of our interactions with angels and guides do not take place in the material world—but rather, within our minds and souls. Since the communication is usually telepathic instead of seen with our eyes or heard with our ears, we may doubt it is real. Suspecting we are just imagining it can be a recurring bugaboo.

As I wrote earlier, we can ask for signs that confirm whatever we discussed with our guides was genuine. This helps us trust we are actually interacting with them. I encourage you to do that whenever you have doubts.

I did this when I felt like I needed help writing about spirit guides in this book. I asked if I could have a specialist guide come to help me. I instantly saw a tall man wearing Victorian garb and a tall top hat step forward. I sensed that he was from England, and I asked if he had owned a house in York, as I intuited. He answered, "Yes, among others." I instantly knew he had been wealthy and was very wise.

His name came to me: Ebenezer. But he told me to call him "Eb." Probably so I'd avoid subconscious negative associations with the famous character of Ebenezer Scrooge from "A Christmas Carol".

That gave me an idea. I asked him to send me a sign: something about or related to Charles Dickens to show up in email, mail, print publications, or social media—-however he could get it to me.

After our conversation, I looked up the meaning of the name Ebenezer. I learned it comes from the Hebrew and means "Stone of Help" or "commemoration of divine assistance," both of which seemed very appropriate for the spirit guide I had asked to assist me.

The day after I met Ebenezer, there was an article on the front page of the digital "Sunday Life" section of the newspaper, that covered a local theater's new adaptation of Charles Dickens' novella, *A Christmas Carol.*

The mention of Charles Dickens was exactly what I had requested to confirm that Ebenezer was indeed my new spirit guide—and he had wasted no time in getting it to me. Could this have been a coincidence? Sure. But in my experience, coincidences are often intentional, not accidental. They frequently have meaning.

The article mentioned that Dickens' novella had been "first published in 1843," and I wondered if the clothing I'd seen Ebenezer wearing dated from that time period. I did a quick Google search—and the images I found did indeed look like his manner of dress: a long tailored frock coat, fitted trousers and a tall top hat.

I had a niggling feeling that Eb may have known Dickens when he had been alive—and ours could turn out to be a very interesting partnership.

PROTECTION FROM UNINVITED SPIRITS

Some people are afraid that if they open themselves up to benevolent spirits, that negative spirits may also show up. Typically, dark spirits are drawn to dark actions and negativity. Unless you deliberately invite them in or do something deleterious (such as the actions mentioned under "Demons"), they won't be attracted to you. However, you can take steps to prevent interactions with spirits you don't want around.

- Specifically ask for the spirits you want to come and communicate with you. I invite my guardian angel and my master spirit guide by name, plus the rest of the spirit guides on my team; these come from God/the Light. I do not just advertise for all spirits to show up when I want guidance. Only ask for those spirits you trust, who you know have your best interests at heart.
- We are all created by God, who is Love and Light. We can repel entities of darkness by turning up the Light of God within us. The spark of our soul is always connected to our Creator. If it were not, we would cease to exist. ("In God we live and move and have our being." as scriptures say.) You can do this by picturing the Light of God as a glowing ball of light in your heart's center. Im-

agine this growing in size and radiance until it fills your body with light. You can even picture the light expanding beyond your body, to fill the room or an entire building. This is the Light of God protecting you. Darkness wants nothing to do with it.

Say NO to the Yes-Yes

If you really want to avoid negative spirits, stay away from Ouija boards.

These "spirit boards" are marketed as games, but that doesn't mean they are harmless. They have numbers, letters, "Yes," "No," and "Good-bye" printed on them. People sit around the board and place their finger lightly on a "planchette" with a pointer that glides around the board to spell out messages from the spirit realm.

"Oui" in French and "ja" in German both mean "yes," so "Ouija" literally means "Yesyes." But this "yes-yes" is a big no-no! The board basically provides a means for any spirit to come through. It's like inviting all of the strangers in a seedy bar to come home with you.

Why would you do that?

Ouija boards often attract negative or low-level entities who are thrilled you have given them permission to invade your space. They will typically lie to you and say that they are a loved one who has passed, or a sweet, innocent child.

If you keep using the board, eventually the spirits' messages may change in character. They may become threatening or direct you to do things that will hurt other people or yourself. These spirits can be very dangerous. They can also attach themselves to you and screw up your life for years afterwards.

Whole books have been written on the disasters that have befallen people who used Ouija boards, and there are many stories online from people who used the board and had truly terrible things happen as a result (including deaths).

Do a little research and you'll want to stay as far away from them as possible.

Some people say Ouija has just gotten a bad rap because it was shown as the cause of the possession in *The Exorcist* movie; but that's really not the case. There is plenty of genuine misery that has come from using the board in the real world.

(By the way, *The Exorcist* was based on a real possession. But if you want to view something even scarier, take a look at the documentary *The Devil and Father Amorth*, by its director, William Friedkin.)

I personally know people who have had very disturbing experiences with the Ouija and now stay as far away from it as possible.

When I was younger, I tried using a Ouija board when I was home alone. At that time, I didn't believe in the board and had no expectation anything would happen. I was just doing it for a lark because I had nothing else to do.

I asked if there were any ghosts around. I was shocked when the planchette started moving swiftly and smoothly on its own. I definitely wasn't pushing it! I couldn't explain how it was moving with my fingertips barely touching the top.

The planchette moved directly to the word "No." That made me laugh. Then who was moving the planchette? I knew it wasn't me.

I suddenly sensed my guardian angel was trying to protect me and saying "No" to my use of the board. I put it away and never used it again.

Unfortunately, there are many people who advocate for the Ouija board, saying "You just have to know how to use it" or "You've just got to close it down properly." This sets people up for dangerous encounters. Even people who think they are experts at preventing Ouija-related problems often experience bad encounters with it.

It's just not worth the risk.

Avoid the Ouija board if you want to prevent negative spirits from coming into your life.

Fortunately, there are other tools that you can use to communicate with your spirit guides that don't pose the same dangers as the Ouija board.

TOOLS TO HELP
YOU COMMUNICATE

If you have silently listened for your master spirit guide's answers to questions but haven't sensed a clear response, you can try connecting with them via spiritual tools. This gives you a very tangible way of interacting with your guides.

Even if you *do* get regular responses and signs from your guides, you may enjoy using these methods. Each provides a different way to communicate that has its own unique benefits and beauty—plus they can help you improve your natural intuition.

Cards for Insight

Every morning I ask my guardian angel and my spirit guides (or simply "my spirit team") to give me their guidance and insight via a single Oracle or Tarot card that I pull for the day. I say, "What do I need to know about today?" or "What should I be aware of today?"

As beings of the light who are here to carry out God's will, helping to prepare us for our day is a task they are happy to fulfill. Make it clear that you are seeking *their* guidance (by name) and no other spirits can come through. You can also surround yourself with a circle of light for extra protection, if you wish.

Many people think that Tarot or Oracle cards are for foretelling the future, but that is not how I use them or how many people today do. Instead, cards can help us tap into the wisdom of our guides—and into our own intuition—so we can make better choices.

Cards can give us insight into the energies we may encounter that day. They can also suggest which challenges we should tackle on any given day. But we always have free will and can choose a different path than a card suggests.

If the card I pick is not as clear as I'd like, I will sometimes pull a second card to clarify the meaning for the day. (I can also simply have a conversation about it with my spirit guides.)

In addition to pulling a daily card, you can pull one or more cards at any time for insight into a decision or action you are about to perform, or about an event or person in your life.

Do not ask "yes" or "no" questions, because YOU are the one who needs to make the decision, not your spirit guides. Instead, ask things such as, "What do I need to know about _____?" or "Give me some insight into this relationship."

If you're torn between two or more things, the cards can also give you a sense of which is better for you. For example, if you're trying to decide between different job offers, you can ask about each one: "What do I need to know about this job offer? What should I know about my potential coworkers? What can you tell me about the boss I would report to? What is important to know about my opportunities for advancement?" or any other questions that will help you decide which offer is ideal for you. Just don't ask, "Should I take this job offer?" because that's a "yes" or "no" question.

I wanted to leave a job that was excruciating, so I pulled a card to see if that was wise. The card made it clear that if I left, I would be unhappy about it. That was not really the message I wanted, but I took my spirit guides' advice and stayed at the job. I was very glad that I did, because the environment at the company soon changed for the better, I got a raise and a promotion—and I stayed in that position for years afterwards.

If you are not familiar with oracle or tarot cards, here's a very quick primer.

Tarot Cards

If you look online or in a local store for a tarot card deck, you will soon see that they can appear very different from each other. That's because as their popularity has proliferated, many artists have created decks. A lot of people now buy tarot decks as much for the artwork as for the usefulness of the cards themselves. (This also leads to people collecting multiple decks. They're hand-sized works of art.)

No matter how different they look, all tarot decks have 78 cards with the same basic meanings—although different guidebooks may put a slightly different spin on the significance of the cards in that specific deck. Any guidebook on the Tarot can usually be used with any deck.

The Major Arcana makes up 22 cards of the deck and represents our journey through life. It contains the dramatic cards you've probably seen in movies, such as "Death" (which usually does NOT mean actual death, but endings), "The Lovers" and "The Tower" (which looks pretty cataclysmic).

The 56 remaining cards form the Minor Arcana, which, like playing cards, have four suits. Here's what each represents (in brief):

- Cups (Water) represent emotions, intuition, love, creativity, fantasy, and relationships.
- Pentacles (Earth) represent money, work, material possessions, nature, family, career, and the physical world.

- Swords (Air) represent intellectual activity, power, communication, conflict, pain, and aggression.
- Wands (Fire) represent action, adventure, energy, ideas, inspiration, spiritual matters, and combativeness.

Cups and Wands have a more optimistic feel overall, while Swords and Pentacles can seem a bit darker.

Each suit includes a Page, Knight, Queen, and King (one more Court Card than in standard playing cards) and ten numbered cards from Ace to 10. Each of these numbered or Court Cards has a basic meaning, which you combine with the symbolism of the suit to get a read on the specific card.

Here are what the numbers represent in general:

- Aces: a gift, opportunity, new beginning
- Twos: partnership, duality, balance, patience
- Threes: creation, fulfillment, relationships, action
- Fours: foundations, structure, home, attachment
- Fives: sorrow, conflict, loss, and change
- Sixes: harmony, well-being, growth, victory
- Sevens: courage, experimentation, attainment, understanding
- Eights: moving forward, mastery, recognition, power
- Nines: perseverance, fulfillment, and fruition of the suit
- Tens: Endings, completion, and achievements related to the suit

Note that the Nines and Tens can be very positive or very negative, depending on the suit.

Here are the basic meanings of the Court Cards:

- Page: Can represent an actual person who is young in years or in spirit. It may also indicate that you are ready and excited for a new opportunity or adventure.
- Knight: Can represent a person of action, who wants to act for the good of others. It may mean that you are taking action to achieve a goal or mission.
- Queen: Can represent a mature woman in our lives. It also represents inspiration, guidance, and leading with inner power instead of brute strength.
- King: Can represent a mature man who is in charge. It also represents dominance, authority, leading with visible power, and the completion of goals.

Like the Minor Arcana, the 22 cards of the Major Arcana have specific meanings. Some people use only the Major Arcana for readings because that's a much smaller deck to deal with, and feels less overwhelming. You can get a general read on what each card means in any tarot book or online.

Here's a very brief guide to the key meanings of the Major Arcana cards (not including reversed meanings, which I don't use).

0 Fool: Innocence, spontaneity, new beginnings, optimism, foolhardiness (leaping before you look)

1 Magician: Creation, action, mastery, power, resourcefulness, manifesting what you need.

2 High Priestess: Intuition, subconscious, going within, wisdom, mystery.

3 The Empress: Creativity, fertility, nurturing, abundance, nature.

4 The Emperor: Structure, discipline, authority, solid foundation, rules, and power.

5 The Heirophant: Institutions, traditions, conformity, guidance, beliefs, religion.

6 The Lovers: Relationships, love, partnerships, choices,

passion, sexuality, union.

7 The Chariot: Progress, movement, determination, willpower, controlling your destiny, victory.

8 Strength: Courage, patience, compassion, power with control (gentle when needed).

9 The Hermit: Meditation, inner wisdom, enlightenment, solitude, introspection, soul searching.

10 Wheel of Fortune: Change, karma, fate, good luck, life cycles, ups and downs.

11 Justice: Fairness, equality, law, balance, cause and effect, truth.

12 The Hanged Man: Surrender, letting go, new perspective, restriction, transcendence.

13 Death: Endings, change, transformation, new beginnings, impermeability.

14 Temperance: Moderation, balance, patience, being sensible, compromise, joining of opposites.

15 The Devil: Feeling trapped, addiction, destructive choices, temptation, materialism, sexuality.

16 The Tower: Chaos, upheaval, disaster, sudden change, release, revelation, instant insight.

17 The Star: Hope, renewal, inspiration, dreams coming true, serenity, believing in yourself.

18 The Moon: Mystery, imagination, dreams, fears, intuition, shadow self, subconscious.

19 The Sun: Happiness, success, joy, fun, positivity, vitality, truth, innocence, all will be well.

20 Judgment: Rebirth, new phase, inner calling, renewal, awakening, absolution.

21 The World: Completion, accomplishment, success, wholeness, attainment, celebration.

Each card can clearly have more than one meaning, so remember to always listen to your intuition when reading tarot cards. It will convey a meaning that's more accurate to your situation than any outside source.

* * *

Although tarot cards have been around for hundreds of years, they didn't really reach their current form until the early 1900's, when tarot expert Arthur Edward Waite worked with artist Pamela Colman Smith to create a deck that set a new standard.

All of the cards in the 1909 deck published by the Rider Company included imagery that gave insight into the meaning of the cards. This was groundbreaking. Before this, most of the cards looked a lot like ordinary playing cards, just picturing what the card was named, such as three cups or seven pentacles, for example.

With the new deck, people could look at the symbols and art on the cards and get a sense of what each one meant without consulting a guidebook.

That original deck has been called various names: the Rider-Waite Tarot deck, Waite-Smith or Rider-Waite-Smith deck, or simply the Rider Tarot deck. It is still in print more than 100 years after it was first published, and it is probably the most widely used tarot deck of all time.

This innovation in tarot made it easier for people to use their intuition with the cards. Many experienced readers actually ignore the "book" meanings of the cards and go with what their intuition says each card means in the context of a reading.

Of course, the cards always rely on your intuition to interpret them as they pertain to your specific situation. For example, if a guidebook says a card means, "You are on track to completing something significant. Remember that you're not alone," you have to decide what it is that you are working on that is important or meaningful to you. It may pertain to your home, your career, a hobby, or a personal goal. The card may also prod you to consult your spirit guides while working on the project, or to ask a mentor for help ("You're not alone").

There are many guidebooks that delve in depth into the

specific meanings of tarot cards or suggest ways to read them intuitively, so I won't go deeply into it. Look in the Resources appendix at the end of this book for suggestions if you are seeking more information.

Oracle Cards

I enjoy using tarot, but I must admit that when I discovered oracle cards, I fell in love. They are modern creations, clearly inspired by the ancient tarot deck, yet they offer a great diversity of artwork, symbols, and meanings.

That's because each oracle deck has been created by an author and/or artist around a specific theme, such as angels, animals, crystals, or the moon. The artwork and cards will all reflect the theme—but that doesn't mean their meanings will be too narrow to be useful. Each deck has wide-ranging messaging that pertains to the situations you may encounter in life.

Overall, oracle card decks tend to be more positive and light-filled than tarot decks, which have cards that convey a lot of dark and negative meanings in addition to the happy, encouraging cards. Some believe tarot is a more accurate representation of the world and our lives in it. But if you want cards that are encouraging and help you to follow a positive path, oracle decks are probably a better choice.

I may pull a tarot or an oracle card, depending on what my intuition suggests for the day. Sometimes I pull one of each. As Halloween approaches, I may pull a card from a Halloween Tarot deck. On the full moon, I may pull a card from a Moon Oracle deck. Do what feels right and appropriate to you.

Sometimes I'll feel drawn to use a card from three different decks (tarot or oracle) for the same day or question, to gain greater depth of insight from multiple perspectives. Or I may draw two cards, one to represent the guidance of my guardian angel and one to provide insight from my master spirit guide.

You can also do card spreads. A "spread" is a specific number and layout of cards chosen from a deck. You can select just three cards, laying them down in a row, or you can create more complex multi-card spreads.

The Celtic Cross spread, for example, includes 10 cards, six laid in a cross pattern, and four cards lined up along the side. I personally don't care for the large, complicated spreads, because I prefer to rely on my intuition more than the cards—and the more cards you lay down, the more divergent messages you will see, so clarity may suffer.

But many people love intricate spreads. You can try one and see if it works for you.

Three Card Spreads

Here are some useful three-card spreads for oracle or tarot cards.

Past. Present. Future.

This may be the most commonly used three-card spread. The first card gives you insight into things that happened in the past that impact your question. The second card gives insight into what is currently happening. This third card gives you a glimpse of a possible future.

For example, say you asked for insight into a relationship. The Past card will give you clues as to what is impacting it; it could be about things you or the other person have said, done or experienced. The Present card may show you elements about your relationship you recognize or have even been trying to ignore. The Future card may suggest how things could proceed if you make no changes.

Problem. Challenge. Solution.

This is another extremely popular three-card spread. The first card, the Problem card, will provide insight into your issue—the actual difficulty may not be rooted in what you think caused it. For example, perhaps it has less to do with the other person, and is more a result of your own attitude. The Challenge card gets to the core of what you are facing. The Solution card suggests a possible avenue you can take to resolve your problem.

More three-card spreads you can try:

- You. Your Relationship. Your Partner.
- Situation. Action. Outcome.
- Mind. Body. Spirit.
- Physical You. Emotional You. Spiritual You.
- Option One. Option Two. Option Three.
- Morning. Afternoon. Evening.
- Worked. Didn't Work. Learnings.
- Strengths. Weaknesses. Suggestion.
- You Can Change. You Can't Change. Go This Direction.
- You. Partner. Children.
- Family. Friends. Partner.
- Guardian Angel Insight. Spirit Guide Insight. Spirit Team Advice.

Obviously, there is an infinite number of ways to set up a three-card spread. Feel free to make up new ones to serve your specific question in the best possible way—always remembering to apply your intuition to what the cards suggest and asking your spirit team to guide you. Remember, the questions you ask should not have a "yes" or "no" answer.

I have asked questions such as "What should I be aware of during the morning, the afternoon, and the evening today (when I'm having dinner with X)?"

When I have clashed with another person, I may ask, "What did I do to contribute to this situation? What did the other person do? What can be done to remedy this?"

* * *

Free-Writing or Speaking With a Card

Give your intuition a chance to shine by riffing on a card. Choose a single card from a tarot or oracle deck. Take a few deep, slow breaths and relax—opening yourself up to your intuition and your spirit guides.

I particularly like to use an oracle deck that has one rather abstract and general word (with many potential "legs") for this type of intuitive work, such as the *Urban Crow Oracle*. This deck has a single word on each card, such as "Battle, Exposed, Fear, Insight, Luck, Memory, Protection, Risk, Survival, Upheaval, Warning, Wrath."

Look at the card in a relaxed state. Handwrite or type whatever pops into your head, sparked by the card. Write quickly to keep your rational mind from taking over and getting sidetracked into thinking. Let your intuition flow. Do NOT try to deliberately generate ideas based on the card. Ideas should just come unbidden into your mind and flow onto the paper via your pen or keyboard.

You can also do this riff on a card without writing, instead speaking aloud for a minute or two as you record yourself. Let your intuition take over and just say whatever comes through.

When you are finished, reread what you wrote or listen to the recording. What has particular meaning to you? Is there some wisdom or advice from the session that you can take into your life? Is anything pointing you in a new direction? If something is intriguing but unclear, ask your guides for clarification.

RUNES REVEAL MORE

Runes offer another satisfying way to connect with your spirit guides. There are 24 symbols in the Elder Futhark, each of which is carved, burned, or imprinted into a small piece of stone, wood, crystal or bone. As you can imagine, rune sets can be very beautiful to look at, even if you never use them!

Just as with tarot or oracle cards, you can use runes to ask for your spirit team's insight into a situation or problem, but again, do not phrase the question in a way that will lead to a "yes" or "no" answer. You're looking for guidance so that YOU can make a decision (not them). Basically, the same guidelines apply to runes as to cards. You can pull a single rune for insight, do a three-rune spread, or more complicated spreads.

So where did runes come from?

Early Norse/Germanic cultures used runes as the letters in their alphabet before Christianity arrived, and runes were eventually displaced by Latin letters. Inscriptions using runes have been found dating back to 150 AD.

The most well-known runic alphabets are the Elder Futhark (the oldest system of runes), the Anglo-Saxon Futhorc, and the Younger Futhark.

There is some evidence that early runes were used for magic or divination, but that doesn't mean they were used exclusively for this purpose. Any system of writing can be used to create spells, but that doesn't make the whole alphabet magical.

J.R.R. Tolkien used Anglo-Saxon runes in his 1937 novel, *The Hobbit*, later creating his own system of runes for *The Lord of the Rings*. Usage of runes in popular culture increased throughout the 20th century, especially in fantasy novels and video games.

Interest in using runes for communication and divination has also expanded, especially in the 1980s, when a number of books and websites on how to use runes appeared.

The Elder Futhark may be the most popular of the runic alphabets used today. There are whole books on how to interpret the runes—but using your intuition in partnership with your spirit team will help you get the guidance that is most specific and perfect for you.

Here is a very condensed guide to the various runes (based on numerous sources). Note that there are three sets of eight runes (aetts) that make up the 24. A few runes have been given different names than the ones listed below, depending on the source, but these seem to be the most common versions.

Freyr's Aett

- Fehu (Cattle): material wealth, prosperity, good luck, abundance, financial success, earned income.
- Uruz (Wild Bull): strength, virility, courage, endurance, health, determination.
- Thurisaz (Thorn/Giants): protection, challenge, danger, conflict, defense, strength.
- Ansuz (Estuary/Message): insight, visions, inspiration,

understanding, wisdom, communication, signs, speech.

- Raido (Wheel/Journey): travel, movement, evolution, progress, decisions.
- Kaunaz (Torch): illumination, knowledge, secrets revealed, creativity, ideas, regeneration, energy.
- Gebo (Gift): exchange, generosity, talents, blessings, partnership, happiness, balance.
- Wunjo (Joy): pleasure, comfort, joy, celebration, festivity, prosperity, harmony, spiritual rewards

Heimdall's Aett

- Hagalaz (Hail): destruction, chaos, sudden and unavoidable change, nature's wrath, being tested, disillusionment.
- Nauthiz (Need): your needs, conflict, restrictions, necessity, lack, endurance, delays, pain.
- Isa (Ice): waiting, delay, blocks, frustration, stillness, inaction, introspection, clarity.
- Jera (Harvest): the year, cycles, fertility, harvest, completion, reaping, abundance, growth, gratitude.
- Eihwaz (Yew Tree): cycle of life, death, dependability, enlightenment, connection, inspiration, sacred knowledge, protection.
- Perth (Dice cup): chance, fate, occult, hidden things, mysteries, secrets, destiny, change.
- Algiz (Elk): protection, defense, guardian, courage, awakening, instinct, strong intuition.
- Sowulo (Sun): joy, abundance, happiness, success, good

luck, health, honor, victory, perfection, wholeness, completion.

Tyr's Aett

- Tiwaz (Tyr/Spear): justice, leadership, honor, bravery, conquest, victory, authority, perseverance.
- Berkana (Birch): fertility, birth, creativity, growth, new beginnings, rebirth, healing.
- Ehwaz (Horse): transportation, moving forward, progress, overcoming barriers, trust, friendship, teamwork.
- Mannaz (Humanity): humankind, the self, identity, relationships, community, society, cooperation, morals and values.
- Laguz (Lake): water, intuition, emotions, dreams, imagination, psychic ability, mysteries, healing, renewal.
- Ingwaz (Fertility): male virility, growth, achieving goals, success, abundance, family, home protection, completion.
- Dagaz (Dawn/Day): breakthroughs, awakening, hope, clarity, illumination, transformation, certainty, completion.
- Othala (Homeland): inheritance, heritage, lasting legacy, ancestry, communal prosperity, possessions, values, the home, death and rebirth.

As you can see from the brief descriptions above, runes have many different possible meanings. This just scratches the surface. Since the meanings are not quite as narrow as those often stated for tarot and oracle cards, your intuition may need to do more of the heavy lifting.

That means runes are not quite as easy to use as cards. If you just want a quick, clear message, you may prefer to consult a tarot or oracle deck. Or you can do what I often do and pick a card for the day, and a rune for the day.

Runes can give you a different perspective on things—and they can be beautiful and fun to use when you want to change things up.

I keep my runes in a cloth bag, so I can shuffle them with my hand while keeping them obscured, until I feel drawn to a specific rune and pull it out. (No peeking!) Then, as always, use your intuition to apply the rune to your specific situation or question. You may pull multiple runes if you feel so directed.

You can purchase sets of runes made of all kinds of materials. I have runes with symbols burned into wood and others inscribed on beautiful stones. You can also create your own runes, writing or inscribing the alphabet on any material you wish, such as rocks you found, card stock, or pieces of wood.

Given the simplicity of the symbols and the smaller number of runes required, it's a lot easier to create your own rune set than your own tarot or oracle deck.

Speaking in symbols

Of course, there's no law that says you must use runes created by someone else to communicate with your spirit guides. You can create your own set of symbols that specifically appeals to you and assign them meanings.

If you like animals, you could create a whole set of animal stones with unique meanings for you. If you like plants, you could draw plant symbols on pieces of wood, or on preserved leaves or paper (which are all made from plants). You could create a whole set with words, with numbers or with the phases of the moon—or you could use a mix of symbols such as a spiral, a rabbit, a crescent moon, a teacup, an oak leaf, anything that speaks to you.

Write down your definitions for each symbol and share it with your spirit guides. Make sure to include a big enough variety of meanings to give your guides sufficient depth to draw from during readings.

When your set is ready, put it in a bag or box. Ask your spirit guides and guardian angel to direct your hand to the one(s) that will provide their advice or insight on whatever you have asked about. Do not look at the symbols until you have pulled them out. As always, use your inner knowing to help you interpret what they mean—and ask your spirit team for guidance.

THE PROBLEM
WITH PENDULUMS

Some people use pendulums in an attempt to connect with spirits. Others say a ghost or spirit flows through your hands to work the pendulum—which makes them similar to the Ouija board, where spirits work through your hands to move the planchette. That would make them dangerous; you don't want to invite spirits to come into your body and manipulate it.

I have always loved rocks since I was a small child, and I was always picking up pretty or interesting stones I found lying around. (My husband will complain that I still do that whenever I'm out walking, sometimes slowing our progress—and even worse, adding to the trove of rocks I already have at home.) So, of course, when I began to purchase beautiful or exotic rocks and crystals, I ended up with a lovely pendulum made of quartz.

I was curious about whether pendulums actually connected with the spirit world or not, so I looked up instructions on how to use one and experimented a little. After a few sessions, my intuition strongly confirmed that the pendulum did not work in that way.

You can see the truth for yourself. Press the end of the chain on your pendulum against a solid surface, such as a counter or table, and let the pendulum hang over the edge. You'll find that it does NOT move when your hand isn't free to make it swing.

I found further proof when I went to a psychic fair. A woman was scheduled to give a presentation on the power of pendulums. All the chairs in the room were full, so I sat on the floor along a side wall near the front. I could see the presenter from the side as she extolled the virtues of pendulums and demonstrated her use of one.

I could also very clearly see that SHE was moving the pendulum back and forth. Her hand and body were moving in the direction that the pendulum swung. No outside force was causing it.

A bunch of teenage girls were so excited by the woman's presentation, they bought pendulums from the vendors at the fair. I hope they didn't put too much faith in what their pendulums later "told" them.

When I took a course in Psychic Development, the well-known psychic teaching the class said that pendulums "do not always work." Even if they "sometimes" worked, it would mean that you could never know when to trust the results of your session with one.

She also told us about being invited to give a presentation at a conference where there were a lot of pendulum devotees. She said that they used them constantly, for everything. Even when going through the line at the café, they would not pick an entrée or a dessert without first whipping out their pendulum to ask which item they should choose. It really slowed things down.

That's pretty silly. But there's one area where pendulums can actually give us insight.

Since we are moving the pendulum ourselves, the answers we get reflect what we subconsciously want or fear. That clarity on what we secretly think, or feel, can be interesting to know about ourselves.

If we are having trouble making a decision, the pendulum may reveal the choice we secretly want to make. This can be helpful if we have been undecided.

However, that doesn't mean we should let our unreliable

subconscious direct the actions of our conscious mind in every situation. In other words, don't immediately rush out to do what the pendulum says you should. If you asked, "Should I quit my job tomorrow?" and it said "yes," that may be what you secretly want, but it's not necessarily what is good for you.

Also, don't trust the pendulum for answers your subconscious doesn't actually know, such as, "Will my baby be born on August 3rd?" Answers to questions like this are more likely to be wrong than right.

Although pendulums can't supply reliable predictions, they do have value as works of art. They can be quite lovely. You could hang them from a chandelier or in a window. Just don't hang your hopes on their accuracy.

The Art of Getting Inside Out

There's another way to find out what our subconscious wants to tell our conscious mind, without the need for a pendulum. This is called "intuitive art", and it uses doodling or scribbling to bring what's inside of us out into the open. It's fun and it's easy. Here's how to do it.

- Choose music you feel drawn to, and play it as you create (this is optional). Don't pick something that's so distracting you end up following the music instead of your intuition. Instrumental music may be "safer" than music with lyrics, which may influence your drawing too much.
- Select a piece of paper (or several sheets) of whatever size and color appeals to you.
- Assemble a bunch of markers, crayons, or pencils in various colors.
- Take a few deep, slow breaths, until you feel relaxed.
- Set a timer for 11 minutes.

- Say, "Intuition, guide me. Flow through me."
- Then just start scribbling or doodling freely. Let whatever wants to show up come out. Do not think about what you're doing or judge it. You're not trying to draw a masterpiece. Moving fast may help you to free your spontaneity. If you feel blocked, say, "Creativity comes through me. Intuition flows freely. There are no mistakes." Let the drawing just happen. Get lost in the process. Have fun!
- When your timer signals the end of the session, look at what you have created. What do you see in your scribbles? Are there any images, symbols, letters, or numbers that have meaning for you? What do the colors represent? Are the shapes you drew angular or round? What emotions do you feel in the art? What does the image evoke?
- You can also ask your spirit guides for insight into the intuitive art.

This is just one tool you can use for enhancing your intuition and creativity, and to help you gain insight into your deeper self.

A PRIMER ON INTUITION

I keep mentioning how you need to trust your intuition and tap into it when communicating with angels and spirit guides. But maybe you're wondering what I mean by "intuition" or are thinking that you are not intuitive. So, let's dive a little deeper into it.

Back when I was a kid (in the Dark Ages) what we would today call "intuition" or "psychic ability" was often termed "extra sensory perception"—or "ESP" for short. That sounds very scientific and in seventh grade, I actually did a science project on it.

I tested people's abilities to "see" one of four different symbols I created that I tried to mentally "send" to them. I discovered that some people correctly "got" the symbols at a far higher rate than one would expect from mere chance. That project earned me a ribbon at the regional science fair.

However, it wasn't until I was an adult that I learned we are *all* intuitive and can actually boost our ability through practice. There are exercises you can do to increase your intuition—but first, let's define the term.

Intuition is "a natural ability or power that makes it possible to know something without any proof or evidence: a feeling that guides a person to act a certain way without fully understanding why" according to Merriam-Webster.

Some people also call this a "hunch," which Merriam-

Webster defines as "a strong intuitive feeling concerning especially a future event or result."

But HOW do you feel this intuitive sense?

It is commonly accepted that there are five psychic senses that correspond to the five bodily senses. Often, a person will receive information most strongly through one or two and less clearly through the others. But we all have the five to a greater or lesser extent. These are often called the "clairs."

Clairvoyance or "Clear Seeing"

This is when you see images or visions in your mind's eye. You may see a picture or moving images, like a video. You may see words. All of this is seen internally, not in your external surroundings. People who are very visual will often have clairvoyance as their dominant psychic sense. "Seeing something" is the ability most people think of first when talking about intuition. You may also have heard of the "third eye" or "second sight."

Clairaudience or "Clear Hearing"

This includes music, spoken words, or sounds that you "hear" internally, not externally. It may feel like telepathy, with someone speaking to you in your mind. For those who love to deal with words or sounds (singers, writers, actors, avid readers), clairaudience may be the dominant psychic sense.

Clairsentience or "Clear Feeling"

This allows you to experience the physical sensations or emotions of another soul. When you get a strong positive or negative feeling about a person or place you've just encountered, you may be sensing the associated emotional energy. It can also be very physical; I once felt pain in my chest when someone mentioned a relative of theirs I didn't know. Then, I learned she had had a heart attack. Very sensitive people who pursue careers as healers or caregivers often have powerful clairsentience.

Clairalience or "Clear Smelling"

This is when you sense aromas, such as the floral perfume or cigar smoke of a person in spirit. The scent is internal; there is no source in the external world. Scientists have found that smelling a scent can evoke a memory very vividly, so spirits may use it to communicate with us. Those who are drawn to working with aromas, such as floral arrangers, perfume makers or cooks, may have a strong sense of clairalience. (Note: Although the other "clairs" have commonly accepted names, people use a variety of terms for this sense, including "clairolfaction" and "clairessence". Pick the one you prefer.)

Clairgustance or "Clear Tasting"

When you suddenly taste something, but you haven't put anything into your mouth, you may be experiencing this "clair." Perhaps a loved one on the other side is sending you a message, reminding you of something they used to cook or share with you. If you have a strong sense of taste and like to cook or bake, you may tap into clairgustance.

Bonus Clair: Claircognizance or "Clear Knowing"

This clair is not associated with one of our five senses. It is when you suddenly "know" something without any conscious information or facts. It may be a premonition about something that will happen in the future or details about a person or event. Because there is no obvious basis for what you suddenly "know," it really requires trusting your intuition.

There are plenty of stories out there about people who felt they shouldn't do something or go with someone and later found out that acting on that sense kept them from a catastrophe (such as becoming the next victim of a serial killer or dying in a car accident after accepting a ride from friends leaving a late-night party).

Many people discount or ignore this clair, because there is no evidence that it is correct in the moment. As a psychic teacher once told me, "Who knows how many people, felt they shouldn't board a plane, but said, 'That's silly,' ignored the feeling, got on the plane, and it crashed."

Intuition often strikes suddenly and without warning, but you can also cultivate it. You can consciously make yourself more open to it—and you can practice using your intuition to strengthen it.

One of the most important things you can do to increase your intuition is to meditate. The very word "meditation" strikes horror into the hearts of many. They think it means clearing the mind of all thoughts—which is close to impossible—and fidgeting silently with increasing boredom and frustration for an hour or more.

Fortunately, that's not necessary, or even very practical. There are many ways to meditate that will help you to both reduce stress and to relax your mind, so you will be more open to your intuition—and clearly receive your spirit guides' suggestions for making life easier.

Tips on that follow.

MEDITATION MADE EASY

Make meditation a habit. That means make it part of your regular day, just like brushing your teeth or making your coffee or tea. Put it on your phone calendar with a reminder to meditate right after you get up in the morning or right before bed—or any other time that works best for you.

Set aside an amount of time you feel you can fit in every day. Maybe it's only five or ten minutes. Fifteen or twenty minutes would be even better if you can do that. But don't feel guilty if you can only commit to five minutes. Try it. You may soon find that you want to spend a longer time in meditation, because of the benefits.

Meditate daily. If you miss a day, don't beat yourself up. Just do it the next day.

Find a quiet place where you won't be disturbed because it can be very distracting when you are trying to concentrate and someone comes in and starts to talk to you or makes a racket in the next room. Tell family members you need a little private time. (I usually meditate before everyone else is up, or when everyone else is gone.)

Make yourself comfortable, with your spine straight. Either sit upright on a chair or lie down. Take three slow, deep breaths.

Relax your body. You can start from the top of the head, gradually relaxing your forehead, your eyes, your cheeks, your jaw, your neck, your shoulders, and on down through your back, arms, fingers, stomach, legs, feet and toes, until you are fully relaxed.

There are several techniques you can try as you meditate. Find out what works best for you or mix it up (for variety). The main objective is to quiet your ego, the part of your mind that is always thinking and worrying about everything, keeping you anxious and on edge. Set a timer for the length of time you plan to meditate (Don't watch the clock). Then use one of the following methods to facilitate your meditation:

Mantra meditation

Choose a word or phrase that has a special meaning to you. It can be the name of your God, such as "Yahweh," "Allah," "Jesus Christ, Son of God," or a religious phrase, such as "Love one another as I have loved you." It can be a word of one syllable, such as "Om," "Ah," "Peace," or "Love." Some people like to use well-known phrases from ancient Sanskrit, such as "Om Mani Padme Hum," which invokes deep compassion. You can also choose an affirmation, such as "I am peaceful," or "I radiate love and light." Mentally repeat your chosen mantra or affirmation over and over as you breathe slowly in and out. You may focus on the first half of a longer phrase as you breathe in and focus on the last half as you breathe out.

Breathwork

Concentrate not on words, but on your breath. This is the very core of life. We can survive for a while without food or water, but we cannot live more than a few moments without breathing. We breathe automatically, usually without noticing it. But when we pay attention to our breathing and even consciously change it, it can be a compelling center for meditation. Here are some methods you can try:

- Focus on the feeling of the air as it enters your body when you inhale, either the sensation at the nostrils, or how it feels as it expands your stomach or lungs. As you exhale, focus on the sensation as the stomach or lungs go flat and/or the breath as it exits your nostrils.
- Count during your inhales and exhales, using one of these methods:
  - Box breath: Slowly inhale to a count of four. Hold the breath for a count of four. Exhale slowly to a count of four. Hold for a count of four. Repeat.
  - Slower exhale: Slowly inhale to a count of four. Pause for a moment. Slowly exhale to a count of six. Repeat.
  - Sevens: Inhale deeply to a count of seven. Hold for a count of seven. Exhale to a count of seven. Repeat.
  - Expanding breath: Inhale to a count of three; exhale to a count of four; Inhale to a count of four; exhale to a count of five. Inhale to a count of five; exhale to a count of six. Continue inhaling and exhaling in this way—always expelling breath for one count longer than the inhale—as you increase the numbers until you finish by inhaling to a count of 14 and exhaling to a count of 15.

You can repeat any of these breath count methods for as long as you feel comfortable. Stop if you feel lightheaded and go back to your normal pattern of breathing.

Focal point

Choose a visual focal point to stare at without thinking. Simply observe it. I sometimes light a candle and stare at the flame. Because the flame flickers, ripples, dances, and changes, it holds the attention of my mind better than a completely still object. But you can choose any object in sight.

How big is the object you are staring at? What color is it? Inspect its every detail. Observe it intensely. It could be something you see every day—yet you may be amazed at how little you have actually noticed about it previously.

Often, we "see" things in our environment without really seeing them. For instance, perhaps your lamp has a nautical scene, but you never noticed the color of the boat before, or how many sails it had. Could you have described the object in great detail to someone before you meditated on it in this way? Probably not.

Mindful Listening

You can focus on other senses to quiet your mind, too. Close your eyes to block out your sense of sight so you can focus better on the sense of hearing. Sit quietly and listen to every sound around you. Notice the roar of cars driving by, sirens increasing and decreasing in volume, birds chirping, a TV or radio in the distance, a dog barking and another answering, your cat scratching in the litter box, neighbors talking outside, wind rustling the trees, the clock ticking—everything your ears can pick up. Stay precisely attuned to any and all sounds. Note them but do not spin off into thinking about their sources.

Bodily Sensations

Focus on how your body feels. Is your scalp itchy? Do your shoulders feel tight? Do you feel an ache anywhere? Carefully note how each part of your body feels. Also note the sensations of your skin where it touches the chair or bed where you are resting. Feel the cushions against your back. If your hands are resting in your lap, feel the double sensations of both your hands and your legs touching each other. Stay deeply focused on your sense of touch, and every sensation in your body.

Repetition

Simple repetitive actions done mindfully, such as knitting, walking, drumming, or using prayer beads (a rosary or mala beads) can help your mind to "zone out" or get "in the flow," preventing you from becoming distracted by your thoughts. You can also receive the benefits of a handknitted scarf, healthy exercise, or answered prayers, depending on your choice of repetitive activity!

Loving Kindness Meditation

This meditation of "metta" or loving kindness, is beloved by Buddhists, and has spread throughout the world among people of all spiritual and religious practices, for good reason. It is less about emptying the mind, than it is about filling one's soul with love.

This raises your spirit into the higher realm of positivity and light—which can also open it up to greater intuition and connection with your spirit guides. Some call this "raising your vibe."

When we remember that we are meant to be Love, we are more able to love ourselves and extend that love to others, even those we may consider "enemies."

There are many different variations on the Metta meditation. Here is one you can try:

Begin by sitting in silence. Take three slow, deep breaths. Consciously relax your body from head to toe. Then set an intention to find the place of loving kindness within you. Speak these words aloud or say them silently inside your head, focusing on the meaning. Pause briefly between each phrase.

May I be happy.
May I be healthy.
May I be safe.
May I be free of mental suffering
May I be free of physical suffering.
May I be at ease.
May I be peaceful.

Repeat these phrases over and over for as long as you feel moved to do so. Then, when you are ready, replace the "I" in each statement with the name of someone you love. You can choose a partner, a parent, a child, a close friend, or a beloved pet. For example, if your loved one is named David, you will say, "May David be happy. May David be healthy. May David be safe," etc. Send these intentions with deep, loving kindness.

Next, bring to mind an acquaintance or someone you don't know well; a person toward whom you feel neutral. It could be the bus driver, a neighbor, a coworker, or the clerk at the grocery store. Set an intention to care for their wellbeing by saying the phrases, either with their name, or with "you" (if you don't know their name): "May you be happy. May you be healthy," and so forth.

Then choose someone who has hurt you or angered you, or with whom you find interactions painful. It could be a difficult boss, an ex, or an estranged relative. If that's too hard, pick someone who annoys you or is bothersome in a minor way. Repeat the phrases with intention to care for this person. You may not feel genuinely loving toward them—but love can be a choice, not an emotion. You are making an effort to transform both yourself and them in a positive way with this practice.

Finally, send loving kindness to all living beings (including animals). "May all living beings be happy. "May all living beings be healthy," etc.

End in silence and take three slow, deep breaths. You may find yourself smiling.

If you want to retain the feeling and the intention of loving kindness during the day after you have finished meditating, you can repeat this affirmation—or you can use it on days when you have not practiced the meditation, to retain the frame of mind evoked by it:

"I practice loving kindness toward everyone, including myself.

Guided Meditations

Guided meditations can be a great way to begin the practice, since they shepherd you through the process. Because they give your mind something to focus on, it is less likely to wander off into a tangle of thoughts.

You can find audible recordings from a wide variety of sources; many are free and others charge for the service. YouTube is a great place to search for guided meditations. I also like the free app, "Insight Timer," which offers lots of options, from guided recordings to sound/music backgrounds that you can set to run for a specific length of time while you meditate.

You may find guided meditations that run from a few

minutes to an hour or more; pick the length and the focus that you prefer when choosing a recording.

Just be aware that if your mind is focused on someone speaking to you through one of these recordings, you are unlikely to hear from your spirit guides while meditating in this way.

* * *

Dealing with distraction

Even experienced meditators will often find their mind spinning off into one thought after another. This has been aptly termed "monkey mind" since thoughts can jump around without stopping, like an energetic monkey.

Don't worry about it. *Don't stop meditating because you start thinking.* When you notice that you are no longer reciting your mantra or paying attention to your breath or focal point, simply redirect your attention back to it.

Give your thinking no more thought—which means don't think to yourself, "I'm no good at this. I can't stop thinking. I can't meditate!" Meditation is not about the complete absence of thought. It's about giving your mind a rest and letting it open up.

Whenever your mind tries to reassert control by thinking, simply notice it and say to yourself, "Thought." Then let it go with a cheery "Goodbye" and return to meditating.

Some people like to imagine their thought as a little cloud drifting through the blue sky and picture it floating away. You can also imagine yourself sitting by a river and whenever you notice a thought, just send it sailing down the river on a tiny boat. Then return to your meditation practice.

There's no need to feel frustrated or think that you're failing at meditation just because you start thinking. Thoughts are a normal and expected part of the process. Don't battle your thoughts. Just send them on their way in a manner that makes you smile. Keep it light. Keep it fun.

Then meditate some more.

ENERGY WORK

Crystals/Stones

Many people believe that crystals and stones carry specific powers and benefits that can assist us spiritually. Others say that's ridiculous.

Since everything is composed of energy, including rocks, it is possible that they may be able to help you tune into different frequencies if you're sensitive to energy. Or stones may just leave you cold.

If you love rocks, as I do, you can try playing around with different ones to see if they enhance your ability to meditate, boost your intuition, or help you communicate better with your spirit guides. If they don't have any noticeable effect for you, at least you'll have a pretty stone to put on your bedside table.

It is possible that the power of rocks could be due to the "placebo effect." That means you perceive they work because you already believe they do. That's not necessarily a bad thing if you get the results you want.

To benefit from stones, you can wear them as jewelry (necklaces, bracelets, earrings, etc.), slip them into your pockets, or place them in your office, by your computer, on a bedside table, under your pillow, or anywhere you want to feel their energy.

There are tons of rocks (literally) out there and lots of books on crystals. Certain rocks are reputed to be good for financial success, health, the immune system, love, luck, etc. Since this book is primarily focused on ghosts, intuition, and communication with your angel and spirit guides, we will concentrate on crystals that are believed to help with that. If you want to know more about rocks that can help you in other areas, look in the Resources section for recommendations.

Here are 21 stones that I recommend if you want to try working with crystals. There's no need to go out and buy them all. Try one in each of the three sections and see if it does anything for you.

Ghosts

These stones won't banish ghosts, but they may protect you from negative vibes and make you feel better in the presence of earthbound spirits. Typically, black stones are believed to be spiritually protective.

Black Tourmaline
Shungite
Black Obsidian
Hematite
Black Onyx
Jet
Smoky Quartz

Intuition/Psychic Ability

Blue and purple stones, which are associated with the Third Eye and Crown Chakras (discussed later in this chapter), are believed to boost intuition and psychic ability.

Amethyst

Lapis Lazuli
Iolite
Sodalite
Blue Kyanite
Labradorite
Blue Apatite

Angel/ Spirit Guide Communication

These stones are reputed to help you raise your vibration, so that you can better connect with angels and spirit guides, and receive their messages more clearly.

Celestite
Angelite
Seraphanite
Amethyst
Selenite
Clear Quartz
Moonstone

In addition to setting stones in a designated spot or in a pocket, you can actively hold them while meditating.

It is believed that your non-dominant hand is the receiving hand, and your dominant hand is the giving/releasing hand. So, if you want to boost your intuition and you are right-handed like me, you could hold an amethyst crystal in your left hand as you quiet your mind. If you want to hear from your guardian angel and spirit guides, you could hold a celestite stone in your left hand while listening quietly for their messages.

If you want to release negative energy, you could hold a black tourmaline stone in your right hand.

If you are left-handed, simply reverse the order of which

hand holds the stones mentioned above.

Of course, I don't always follow the "right/left" suggestions; I often wear stone pendants that are centered on my neck or chest, and I almost always wear crystal bracelets on my left wrist (since I'm right-handed, I don't want bracelets to get in my way).

It helps if you set a specific intention or desire as you are holding, carrying, or wearing your crystal. Think about your intention occasionally during the day and restate it in your mind as you touch your crystal.

Believe in it. This will help you to achieve it.

FUN FACT: Window glass is made by heating sand, which is made primarily of quartz. So, can gazing through windows give us the same benefits as staring at a clear quartz crystal ball?

Chakras

Many mediums and meditators focus on the life force energy in our body known as "prana," which is the word for "breath" in Sanskrit. Our breath not only keeps us alive, it can help us balance our energy and emotions.

Many people have felt the calming power of focusing on breathing slowly in and out. But there's much more you can do to calm and center yourself by focusing on the energy inside your body.

"Prana" energy flows through your body in various channels. The most powerful connection points and foci of this energy are the chakras.

"Chakra" comes from the ancient Sanskrit of India and means "wheel." Chakras are the energy centers of the body, which are envisioned as spinning circles of energy that affect us spiritually, emotionally, and physically. When our chakras are open and aligned, energy can flow through them, and we experience harmony in mind, body and spirit.

There are seven main chakras in the body that are the primary focus among most practitioners in the western world. They run from the base of the spine to the top of the head.

The colors associated with the chakras reflect the visible spectrum of light, in order: red, orange, yellow, green, blue, indigo, violet. The crystals associated with each chakra are those that match the color of the chakra.

Here is a quick guide to the chakras. (You can read whole books on them and go more in depth, if you are interested.) Following this, you will find ways to use the colors and musical notes listed below to help you balance each of your chakras.

Root Chakra (Muladahara)

This is located at the base of the spine and helps us to stay strong and grounded. When it's in balance, it gives us a feeling of energy, health, and stability. When it's unbalanced, we may feel fearful, anxious, and insecure. Color: Red. Seed Sound: Lam. Musical Note: C. Affirmation: I am.

Sacral Chakra (Svadhishthana)

This is located a little below the belly button and is the center of our creativity and sensory pleasures (including sex). When it's in balance, we feel joyful, creative, and live life to the fullest, reveling in our senses. When it's unbalanced, we may feel stifled, have less joy and sex drive, or be over-focused on sex and pleasures, which can lead to destructive addictions. Color: Orange. Seed Sound: Vam. Musical Note: D. Affirmation: I feel.

* * *

Solar Plexus Chakra (Manipura)

This is located right in your stomach or "gut" (where we get our "gut feelings"). When it's in balance, we feel powerful, confident, strong, and courageous, and we tackle our goals with vigor. When it is unbalanced, we may feel weak, powerless, with low self-esteem, often resulting in anger and lack of progress toward our goals. Color: Yellow. Seed Sound: Ram. Musical Note: E. Affirmation: I do.

Heart Chakra (Anahata)

This is located in the center of the chest, and is considered the center of our being, where all energies meet. When it's in balance, we feel love for ourselves and others, and we feel loved and happy. When it's unbalanced, we feel fearful that we will never be loved in a deep and satisfying way, and we may have trouble extending love to others. Color: Green. Seed Sound: Yam. Musical Note: F. Affirmation: I love.

Throat Chakra (Vishuddha)

This is located at the throat and is the first of the upper chakras. It is focused on communication. When it's in balance, we are able to express ourselves and listen to others better; we can let go, forgive and move forward. When it's unbalanced, we may have trouble expressing ourselves, and guilt and shame may keep us from listening well or remaining present. Color: Blue (usually light blue). Seed Sound: Ham. Musical Note: G. Affirmation: I speak.

* * *

Third Eye Chakra (Ajna)

This is located in the center of our forehead, just above and between our eyes. It is the source of our intuition. When it's in balance, our psychic ability is strengthened, we develop spiritually and see the world with understanding; we feel inner calm and peace. When it's unbalanced, we may have trouble making sense of life. When it's overactive, we can become overwhelmed. Color: Indigo. Seed Sound: Om. Musical Note: A. Affirmation: I see.

Crown Chakra (Sahasrara)

This is located at the top of the head and connects directly with the Divine, representing enlightenment. When it's in balance, we find transcendence, receiving illumination from the Divine, and awakening to the fact that we are connected to everything in the universe (All is One). When it's unbalanced, we may feel unstable and even crazy, or experience painful migraines. Color: Violet. Seed Sound: Om. Musical Note: B. Affirmation: I understand.

How to balance your chakras

There are many different techniques to balance your chakras. Here are a few:

- Use the Colors of the Chakras. Imagine a spinning wheel of red light at the base of your spine. Breathe slowly and deeply as you see it spin and brighten until it feels balanced. Next, see a spinning wheel of orange light under your belly button. Breathe slowly as you see it spin and brighten until it feels balanced. Move up the chakras in this way, picturing spinning wheels of light in the colors of the chakras at their points on the body. Envision yellow at the solar plexus, green at the heart, light blue at the throat, indigo at the third eye, and violet at the very top of your head—until you see all your chakras lit up and spinning. Sit with this for a while and enjoy the feeling. Then, gently quiet them; slow the spinning and let the colored lights dim. Take a deep breath and let your image of the chakras fade. Take another deep breath and you are ready to face the world.

- Use the Sounds of the Chakras. If you have Tibetan or crystal singing bowls, sound them one by one as you gradually move from the "C" note of the root chakra to the "B" note of the crown chakra. Spend time with each note and do not move on until you feel that the associated chakra is balanced. If you don't have bowls, you can find videos on YouTube that will play the notes for you. (Such as "Crystal 7 Bowl Chakra Set Notes CDEFGAB")

- Use the Crystals of the Chakras. While meditating on the colors of the chakras, you can hold corresponding crystals of the associated colors to boost the effectiveness. You can also wear bracelets, pendants or earrings with the seven chakra colors to help you feel more balanced. (Right now, I'm wearing an aventurine point with seven chakra colors attached to it in order.)

The Psychic and Spirit Communication Chakras

The upper chakras (Throat, Third Eye and Crown) are particularly helpful in boosting your intuition and communicating with angels and spirit guides. So, spend time opening those particular

221

chakras if you want to enhance your intuitive abilities, receive messages from loved ones who have passed, or hear from your spirit guides. Gently close your chakras when you want to go back to your regular day.

Some people also focus on the solar plexus chakra, where we can get an intuitive "gut feeling" about something.

BOOSTING YOUR INTUI-
TION

Many people say, "I'm not psychic, but I have a feeling that I should check on my mom," or "I don't think I should take the bus today." Trust those feelings. You actually ARE psychic. Everyone is, to a lesser or greater extent. But since there's a lot of baggage with the word "psychic," let's talk about your intuition (which is really the same thing).

You can strengthen your ability over time by practicing tapping into your intuition. There are an almost infinite number of ways to do this. Simply ask a question that requires you to "get" or "know" the answer without using your usual senses.

Here are some techniques and exercises to start you out—but I encourage you to think up your own unique ways to practice being intuitive as you go about your daily life.

Stoplight

Think of a question you have that requires a "yes" or "no" answer. You could ask, "Is this choice for my highest good?" Then close your eyes and imagine a stoplight in front of you. What color is the stoplight? Green means "yes/go ahead," Red means "no/stop," and yellow means to "act with caution/wait."

If you don't see a light, let one of the words green, red or yellow pop into your head.
Two Paths

If you're trying to decide between two choices, close your eyes and imagine two paths diverging in front of you. Have one path represent one of your choices and the alternative path represent the other. Walk down the first path. How does it feel? Is it beautiful? Is it raining and cold or sunny and warm? Is it an easy walk, or is it rough going? Then go back to the fork and walk down the other path. How does that one feel? Compare it to the first path. This can help you decide between the two.

Colors

Choose a person, such as your boss, a coworker, friend, relative or neighbor, and ask yourself what color he or she will be wearing tomorrow. Were you right? Keep trying, and you may find that your accuracy improves.

Mail

When you get a bill in the mail, ask yourself what number will be on the invoice. If you receive a sales or fundraising letter, ask yourself the name of the person who signed the letter. Then open the envelopes and check your accuracy. Don't worry if you're not spot-on. Practice makes perfect.

Emails

In the morning, predict how many emails you will get before you open your mail account. Then guess the first word you will see in the title of the first email. You can do this every morning before you look at your emails.

Dice

Before you shake one or two dice, ask yourself what number will come up. This can be a lot of fun. Keep track of your results. How many times were you right after 10 or more rolls?

Cards

Shuffle a standard deck of playing cards. Then use your intuition to determine what the top card will be. If identifying one specific card out of 52 seems too tough, you can start by asking yourself for the suit or number of the top card. Then turn it over. Keep track of your results. Do you see an improvement over time?

Practice With Someone You Trust

It's not unusual to have a psychic connection with someone who is dear to you. You may correctly sense when a loved one who lives far away is in trouble. You may instantly know that a particular friend is calling you on the phone, even before you look at the name of the caller.

These near and dear people can make good subjects for exercising your intuition. If you don't already have this kind of special connection with a friend or relative, you may be able to build a bond with someone who shares your interests.

All you need is a person that you trust who is willing to partner with you in practicing the use of intuition. Working with another person is one of the most enjoyable ways to learn how to boost it.

You can practice while you are in the same physical location, or do it remotely, using video apps, emails, phone texts, or calls. (Many psychics and mediums today give readings via video apps or phone calls because there are no geographical limitations to intuition.)

Here are some starter ideas for practicing with a partner:

First, clear your mind and relax. Don't try too hard. That will just stress you out and make you less accurate. Remember, this is meant to be fun!

Second, trust what you see or "get." It may be an image, a word, a number or a symbol. We often second-guess ourselves. We think it's just our imagination. It's not. Tell yourself, "I am intuitive, and I trust what I get."

Third, don't feel embarrassed if you don't get something "right." Just keep practicing. Even the most famous psychics and mediums don't achieve 100% accuracy!

First Name Reading

Ask your partner to give you the first name and first initial of the last name of someone they know that you do NOT. Also give them a first name and initial of the last name of a person you know that they do not. It's important that you both pick a person that you know very well—because otherwise you won't be able to truly evaluate the accuracy of what each of you shares.

Now ready yourselves to intuitively read the person that your partner named. Quiet your mind and see what comes to you.

If you don't get anything, try prodding your intuition by asking yourself specific questions such as: Is the person young or old? Are they related to my partner? What do they look like? What do they do for a living? What are their hobbies? Where do they live? Do they have pets; what kind? What is their personality like? You may see images, hear phrases or words, see colors or numbers, hear a last name, smell or taste something, feel sensations in your head or chest that indicate an illness or injury.

Sometimes images can be metaphors for something else. An apple may represent that the person is a teacher. A chicken may suggest that the person is afraid of something. On the other hand, an apple may more directly signal that the person owns an apple orchard, and a chicken may tell you that they raise chickens.

Write down *everything* that your intuition gives you, even if it doesn't seem to make sense.

After a set amount of time (such as three-to-five minutes), tell your partner what you have received intuitively. Find out what resonates and what does not. If something doesn't seem to fit but you feel strongly about it, ask them to remember it and see if it makes sense later. (Sometimes, people forget little pertinent details in the moment that would confirm your accuracy.)

Pay careful attention to what your partner tells you they received for your named person. Does it resonate in a direct way or a symbolic sense? If they give you a last name, does it fit the person or anyone close to them? If they get a number, how is it significant to them (if at all)? Is it the age of the person, the month that they were born or died, the number of kids they have, their birth order?

Whenever you practice with your partner, make note of everything that makes sense and anything that doesn't. You are likely to find that your accuracy improves over time.

You may also notice that certain symbols come up repeatedly—and signal the same meaning for different people. This can help you build a library of psychic shortcuts that you can refer to as you move forward.

Unseen Photo Reading

Pick out a photo of someone you know well and ask your partner to do the same. If you are practicing together in person, bring the photos in envelopes so that the other person cannot see yours.

Each of you will try to "read" the unseen photo intuitively, writing down everything that comes to you in three-to-five minutes. Use the same methods and prompts mentioned in the previous practice exercise. Be sure to write down what you get.

When the time is up, share what you received about the person in the photograph.

You can also choose photos of places instead of people and ask each other to describe the place in the unseen photo. Intuitively, try to determine whether the place is tropical, temperate, or arctic. Is it summer or winter in the photograph? Is there water somewhere in the picture? Are there forests or mountains? Is it a city with tall buildings or way out in the country? Is there a house or neighborhood? Are there people, animals, or vehicles in the shot?

Share what you each received and evaluate your accuracy. Pay attention to the different meanings your intuitive insights can have. For instance, if you get the number "three" are there three people or three houses in the photograph? Is a child in the photograph age three?

Always listen to your intuition as you assess the results of your intuitive exercises. Your "inner knowing" does not function like your rational mind. Its symbols may connect in an intuitive way, not necessarily in a logical manner.

Color Reading

If you want to start with something simpler than reading a person or a place, try sending each other a specific color. You could restrict yourself to using the spectrum: red, orange, yellow, green, blue, indigo, violet. These are also the colors of the chakra energy centers that run from the base of our spines to the top of our heads.

Have your partner focus on a picture or object of a specific color and try to intuitively get the color your partner has chosen. What image pops into your mind? Do you see the name of the color? Do you see an object of that color? Do you feel an emotion that is tied to the color? Write it all down.

Then reverse the process. Focus on a color and let your partner practice their intuition. Since this shouldn't take as long as the more complex exercises previously mentioned, you should be able to do several sets of psychic color readings in one sitting. Make sure that you both do the unexpected; don't just go through all the seven colors of the spectrum in order. Jump around and even repeat colors so that each person can't simply guess what the next color might be.

Instead of limiting yourself to the spectrum, you could instead choose to use an infinite number of colors, opening the door to hues such as burgundy, turquoise, chartreuse, pale pink, blue-green, silver, black, etc. Focus on a picture or object in the unique color that you are trying to send, to give the receiver the clearest image and the best chance of reading it.

Song Reading

Have you ever had a song title pop into your head just before you turned on a radio or walked into a store—and then, surprise—you heard the song playing? This used to happen to me a lot when I was a young teenager.

There was a radio on the nightstand next to my bed and I loved to listen to the latest hits. When I reached out my hand to turn on the radio, often a title would come into my head. As soon as the radio was turned on, that song would be playing. It was never a tune that was particularly special to me—and it wasn't the same piece over and over; the title varied.

This amazed me. I wondered how I knew the song that was going to be playing at that very moment. When I tried to mentally will myself to "know" the next hit that would show up, it didn't work. The correct song title only came to me when I wasn't trying.

Maybe this kind of thing can happen to us because music has a unique power. It can transform our emotions, making us feel like dancing for joy, or weeping with sadness. Special songs can bring us back to another time and place, jogging important memories.

Music, both instrumental and with vocals, is also an integral part of most religions and celebrations. We sing "Happy Birthday" for loved ones and Christmas carols during the holidays. "Take me out to the ball game" unites us as we cheer for our home team. "Auld Lang Syne" has become a tradition around the world at New Year's.

The Pythagoreans thought there was "music of the spheres" produced by the vibration of the celestial spheres that created a cosmic, ethereal harmony. Even the angels in heaven are believed to spend a lot of time singing.

Because music is so powerful, it can be a strong focus for an intuitive exercise with your partner. Before you get together (in person or remotely), choose several songs that you would like to send to your partner. Have them do the same.

You may want to choose some songs that evoke strong emotions to see if those are easier for the other person to pick up. Select neutral or simply pleasant songs, too.

Take turns sending and receiving each song. When sending to your partner, concentrate on the song title—and if possible, have the song playing on your earbuds. (Make sure your partner can't hear it.)

If either of you intuitively gets any of these, consider them "hits": the full song title—this is obviously the strongest "hit"; key words from the title (not "the"); bits of lyrics; the name of the band or soloist singing the song; snippets of the melody; knowledge of the arrangement or instrumentation; the musical style (rock, jazz, opera, pop, rap, etc.).

It requires intuition to get these with any accuracy (unless you have each picked your favorite songs and the other person knows what your faves are—avoid that)!

It may be easier to "get" a song being sent if you are already familiar with it—but maybe not. Experiment and see.

You can also practice intuitively receiving song titles without a partner. Sit in a comfortable place next to a radio or digital source of streaming music. Or try it when you're driving in a car. The mind often zones out a bit when driving, and there's usually a radio you can turn on if a song title pops into your head.

Unlike my adolescent attempts, don't try to will yourself into getting a song title. The trick is to clear your mind. Relax. Try not to think. Try not to try at all. See if anything shows up. If you get a song title, turn on the radio.

If it's playing, you got a hit. If it's not, turn off the radio and try again.

Other things to try

You can also experiment with intuitively sending and receiving these with a partner:

- Objects
- Book Titles
- Movie Titles
- Addresses
- Money (coins and paper money)
- Animals
- Days of the week
- Months of the year

- Dates: you could leave off the year and just do the month and day, such as May 11th, or you could add the year for extra difficulty: May 11th, 1878.
- Chakra centers (if you're both familiar with them)
- Anything else that appeals to you that you would like to try!

Is It Just a Thought or Is It Genuine Intuition?

Intuition is a subtle science. It can often be hard to distinguish between your own thoughts and intuitive information. Here are some ways to differentiate the two:

- Ego-generated thinking is driven by desires, emotions, knowledge, beliefs, and expectations. These thoughts typically reinforce our existing opinions and convictions, or they may reflect our fears. We may get emotional about a stream of self-created thoughts, but they don't give us surprising new information or tell us anything that we don't already know.
- Intuitive thoughts are not created from the ego, so they will feel neutral and unemotional. They often just pop into your mind. Because they don't stoke strong feelings, we may not pay close attention to them. If your intuition knows that something could be important to you, the intuitive thought may recur or become repetitive, always with a calm, unemotional tone. For example, you may think, "I should take a new route on my daily walk." but it's easier to just do the established route, so you don't. The next day you feel the urge to turn down a different street than usual and you finally follow that thought. You hear someone call your name. A woman jumps out of a car and it's a good friend from high school that you lost track of, and haven't seen in years.

You had been trying to find her on Facebook, albeit unsuccessfully, because she's married now and you only knew her maiden name. It was your intuition that put you on the road that would lead you to her. (Something like this happened to me.)

Classes and Workshops

If you want to take the development of your intuitive or psychic ability up a notch, you can go beyond practicing alone at home or with people you already know. You can join others around the world on Facebook sites that let you practice your psychic or mediumistic ability. These can be very helpful. Just make sure that you agree with the policies and approach of the administrators before signing up.

I am a member of a Facebook group where people post photographs and invite everyone to use their psychic ability—or medium ability if the person in the photo is deceased—to read the person, animal, or object in the photograph. Everyone who wants to participate posts what their intuition told them about it. The person who posted the photograph will then let everyone know what was accurate and what was not.

Another Facebook group I love holds live Zoom sessions to educate members and also to do development circles for practicing and improving evidential mediumship.

You may find groups like these very helpful, especially if you don't already know someone you can practice with. They are usually free, too!

Many psychics and mediums—including household names—also offer online classes on developing your psychic or mediumistic ability. Don't get starry-eyed by famous teachers, though. Make sure to vet the program before spending any money on it. Many of these courses cost hundreds of dollars. You may find that lesser-known psychics or mediums can be better teachers, and their courses are likely to cost less.

Talk to people who have taken the course that interests you. Did they think it was worth it? What did they learn? Do they feel that the course enhanced their abilities? Also look at people's comments and their ratings of the teacher and the class.

If you are fortunate enough to live in an area where there are well-regarded professional psychics, or where renowned traveling psychic mentors come through, you may be able to take in-person courses or workshops from these experts. I highly recommend that.

Do the same vetting process for in-person classes as you would for online classes. I talked to people who had taken the course, liked it, and could give me insight into it, before I signed up for an in-person, 16-week class called "Psychic/Spiritual Development." It was taught by a local psychic who is nationally known (she has been in the field for decades, has appeared on TV, written numerous books, and hosted podcasts). I thought it was excellent!

The class was pay-as-you-go because the psychic had found that many people would come for one or two sessions out of curiosity. and then drop out. Also, sometimes people would quickly feel that they had NO psychic ability and were too embarrassed to continue when they couldn't "get" anything.

I didn't miss a single class, even though it was a long drive from work and it stressed me out trying to get there on time in the early evening. I learned a lot, gained new contacts, and had fun.

The psychic would sometimes bring in other experts to talk about things such as auras, ghosts, and past lives.

But the most exciting part of each class was the psychic exercises we practiced with different partners every week. Because we, as classmates, didn't know each other before we had signed up, it worked well.

With each exercise, we worked on intuitively receiving information for a couple of minutes, writing down what we got.

Then we shared it with our partner. Sometimes it was surprising what the correct images meant.

Early on, I quickly got the last name of a person my partner wanted me to read. That was exciting. Another time, I got the name "Richard," and my partner said that every single one of her exes had been named Richard.

When we were practicing mediumship, one of my partners insisted on telling everyone in class that I had said the exact same thing about her deceased husband in heaven as a professional medium she had consulted. Another time, my partner told me that every single thing I had mentioned about her deceased loved one was correct. All of these correct "hits" encouraged me.

However, I also often got things that didn't resonate with people. We all did. Our teacher said to look at whether what we got could be symbolic instead of literal, but most of us focused on literal meanings during the class. It takes time to develop an understanding of what the signs and symbols you get might mean beyond their literal significance.

Earlier that same year, I also took a weekend workshop from two highly respected evidential mediums, who had traveled to my city for the event. The workshop was on connecting and working with your spirit guides.

That was when I first met my master spirit guide and learned how to ask my guides for proof or confirmation of the truth of messages that I believed I had received from them. That was invaluable.

Books and Websites

There are a huge number of books out there on ghosts, hauntings, and ghost hunting. Many perpetuate myths, hearsay and inaccuracies about ghosts and present earthbound spirits as terrifying. Maybe this helps sell books, but in my opinion, it is a disservice to the reader and to the spirits as well.

Ghosts can be annoying, but they are not usually the demonic horrors that some people make them out to be. Our perception colors what we see.

However, there are some wonderful books on ghosts; see my Resources section near the end of this book for recommendations. I also suggest some excellent websites and some Facebook pages you may want to peruse.

In addition, my Resources section lists good books and websites for learning more about angels, spirit guides. and intuition. Many of these were created by psychic mediums that I believe are trustworthy.

Evidential mediums who have been double-blind-tested or triple-blind-tested by scientists or reputable organizations are the ones that I would recommend over those who simply put up a shingle and say they're a psychic medium. (Do NOT go on psychic phone lines.)

Anyone can put up videos on TikTok, Instagram, and YouTube and claim to be a psychic. That doesn't make them legitimate. The advice they give may not be good or helpful. Follow only those people you have reason to trust.

WHY ARE WE HERE?

From an early age, I felt that we were on earth for one main purpose: to learn how to love ourselves, each other, and God—unconditionally. It sounds simple, but it's something I'm still working on.

It can be very hard with all of the cruelty, abuse, violence, war, heartless pollution, divisions, anger, fear, and "I'm right and you're not" opinions found everywhere on this planet, spread far and wide on social media.

The chaos seems never ending. But our time in this material world is actually very short. As you get older and the days remaining are far fewer than the ones you've already experienced, you come to understand that.

Many people call our time here "Earth School" and say it's one of the toughest classrooms in the universe. Others say that our souls came here for an exciting adventure vacation away from the tranquility of Heaven. I personally think it's a spiritual version of "Study Abroad," combining deep learning with thrilling new experiences.

Whether we actually chose to come here or were sent here for our own good is up for debate.

But remember that you are never alone. You are loved and supported by God, your guardian angel, and a whole spirit guide team.

Everything that happens in our life provides an opportunity

for us to learn and grow. Even tragedy.

Especially tragedy.

Gradually, if we mature, we find that it is always better to choose love over fear.

One of my very favorite quotes, from the brilliant and insightful Franciscan, Richard Rohr, helps me to remember a shining truth that can get us through even difficult days. It's so wonderful that I asked my talented goddaughter/niece Marie to stitch it up for me.

"Love will always win. God does not lose."

In the end, remember that. No matter how much hatred and fear seem to rule the day, eventually Love will have its way.

May your life be filled with hope and love.

RESOURCES

There is a lot to pick from out there, ranging from terrific to terrible. These are some of the sources I recommend.

Books

Many of the authors listed here have written multiple books, but I did not include more than two by a single author. If you like their first book, you are likely to enjoy their others. Consider this a starting point.

On Ghosts

Ghosts: True Encounters with the World Beyond, Hans Holzer
When Ghosts Speak, Mary Ann Winkowski
The Ghost Photographer, Julie Rieger

On Signs from Departed Loved Ones

Hello From Heaven, Bill and Judy Guggenheim
Signs, Laura Lynne Jackson

On Meditation

Secrets of Meditation, davidji

On Intuition/Psychic Ability/Mediumship

A Still, Small Voice, Echo Bodine
Speaking the Language of Intuition, Jodi Livon
Infinite Quest, John Edward
Messages From Above, Monica the Medium
The Light Between Us, Laura Lynne Jackson
Messages of Hope, Suzanne Giesemann
Still Right Here, Suzanne Giesemann
A Psychic's Life, Michael Bodine
Psychic Navigator, John Holland
There's More to Life Than This, Theresa Caputo
You Can't Make This Stuff Up, Theresa Caputo
Psychic Living, Stacey Wolf

On Spirit Guides

Let Your Spirit Guides Speak, Debra Landwehr Engle
Wisdom From Your Spirit Guides, James Van Praagh

On Demons

The Demonologist: The Extraordinary Career of Ed and Lorraine Warren, Gerald Brittle
Hostage to the Devil, Malachi Martin

On Tarot

Everyday Tarot, Brigit Esselmont (Founder of Biddy Tarot)
The Complete Illustrated Guide to Tarot, Rachel Pollack

On Runes

The Runes: A Human Journey, Kari C. Tauring
Runes Illustrated: How to Read Them. Rachel Newcombe

On Crystals

The Illustrated Directory of Healing Crystals, Cassandra Eason
Crystals, Jennie Harding

On Chakras

Chakras for Beginners, David Pond

Tarot and Oracle Decks

There are a vast number of options out there. Here are some of my favorites. Note that I have again limited each author to two decks under each category. Some (such as Colette Baron-Reid, Denise Linn, and MJ Cullinane) have numerous wonderful decks, so if you love these, you'll probably love their other decks too.

Tarot

The Good Tarot, by Colette Baron-Reid
Guardian of the Night Tarot by MJ Cullinane
The Grimalkin Tarot, by MJ Cullinane
The Halloween Tarot, by Kipling West

Oracle

Wisdom of the Oracle, by Colette Baron-Reid
The Spirit Animal Oracle, by Colette Baron-Reid
Moonology Oracle Cards, by Yasmin Boland
The Sacred Forest Oracle, by Denise Linn
Sacred Traveler Oracle, by Denise Linn
Queen of the Moon Oracle, by Stacey Demarco
Seasons of the Witch: Samhain Oracle, by Lorriane Anderson and Juliet Diaz
Urban Crow Oracle, by MJ Cullinane
Divine Intuition Oracle, by Belinda Grace

Spirit/Medium Decks

Messages from the Guides Transformation Cards, by James Van Praagh
The Spirit Messages Daily Guidance Oracle Deck, by John Holland
The Mediumship Training Deck by John Holland and Lauren Rainbow

Paranormal Events

To get the most up-to-date listings, search online for "Paranormal events and conventions {YEAR}" or "Ghost events and conventions {YEAR}" or "Psychic events and conventions {YEAR}" and you'll find the most current opportunities, featuring celebrities, presentations, and vendors in the paranormal field.

Websites

The authors mentioned above all have associated websites. Many of them are primarily focused on selling their products (books, readings, classes). Here are a few I frequent for their resources and links to events.

suzannegiesemann.com
colettebaronreid.com
maryannwinkowski.com

Facebook Groups

The first two Facebook pages below contain posts from people who believe they are experiencing haunting. They are very interesting and entertaining. The other three are practice groups for boosting your mediumship or psychic ability.

This Old Haunted House
True Ghost Stories
Development Practice Circles for Evidential Mediumship
Mediumship Development & Psychic Training Group—Pathway of Light
All Things Spirit: Psychic, Medium & Intuitive Development and More

YouTube Video Channels

These feature mostly "talking head" videos, but they are very informative and interesting.

Mary Ann Winkiowski (about ghosts and related topics)

Suzanne Giesemann (about the afterlife and communicating with the deceased)

James Van Praagh (psychic mediumship and spirituality)

The Paranormal 60 with Dave Schrader (entertaining news, interviews, discussions)

Medium Charlie Kelly (UK Medium, Training for being a medium)

Martin Twycross Medium & Teacher (UK Medium, teaches how to do it)

Tony Stockwell (UK Medium, guided meditations for spirituality, meeting angels, developing mediumship)

"Be Psychic, 4 Steps, 5 Minutes" Stacey Wolf James—a fun, quick video to instantly tap into your psychic abilities

Podcasts

Spooked (True ghost & paranormal stories told by those who experienced them)

Real Life Ghost Stories (True ghost stories sent in by listeners and read by the host)

Uncanny (BBC podcast featuring true paranormal stories and disagreeing skeptics)

Radio Rental (Real life horror and paranormal tales told by those who survived them)

Otherworld (True paranormal tales told by experiencers engaging with the host)

Education/Courses

Arthur Findlay College (UK) is perhaps the most widely known school for psychic mediums. Courses used to be taught entirely in person, but now the school offers many online courses at arthurfindlaycollege.org.

Echo Bodine has been teaching in person "Psychic Development" and other courses for decades. She now offers classes online, so you can learn from her no matter where you live. She has written numerous books, as well. See echobodine.com.

Suzanne Giesemann offers in-person classes and workshops as well as online courses and mentoring, focused on developing evidential mediumship. See suzannegiesemann.com.

James Van Praagh School of Mystical Arts offers online video courses in spirituality, psychic and mediumship development. See jvpschoolofmysticalart.com.

John Holland Webinars and Videos on developing psychic and mediumship abilities are available at johnholland.com.

Organizations

The Society for Psychical Research (UK) was the very first organization founded to conduct scholarly research into the paranormal. It has been around since 1882. Visit them online at spr.ac.uk.

Collecting Material Ghosts

I used to buy ghosts, witches, monsters, and vampires as part of my Halloween decorations (I overdecorate for every major holiday). But eventually, as real ghosts became a genuine part of my life, my instinct for collecting kicked in, and I bought tiny ghost figurines that I could keep out year-round.

I have amassed a small collection. The tallest one, made of blown glass, is around 4"; all of the rest are smaller. Several are carved from beautiful stones, one is a tiny marbled synthetic spirit, and the rest are phantoms made largely of gypsum, handcrafted by The York Ghost Merchants in the UK.

Their charming ghosts are one-of-a-kind and highly sought after. Every edition sells out instantly. I currently have five of their phantoms. You can find them on social media and at yorkghostmerchants.com. Their Victorian-flavored website is a delight in itself.

GHOSTS, GUARDIANS & GUIDES IN YOUR LIFE

Have you ever had a paranormal experience?
Has your guardian angel saved you from disaster or death?
Have you received signs from loved ones or spirit guides?

I'd love to hear about it!

Please share your experiences on my Facebook page, Collecting Spirits: Ghosts, Guardians & Guides and/or on my Instagram @collectingspirits_ghosts

ACKNOWLEDGMENTS

There are many, living and dead, that I want to thank:

David, for not thinking (or at least not saying out loud) that I was crazy when I first told him about the poltergeist, and who patiently let me drag him to countless haunted sites. Thanks also, for reading this book and encouraging me to get it out there.

Yvonne, my sister, who joined me on Zoom and drove us halfway across the country to meet the ghost medium, bringing two earthbound spirits along with us.

All the people who trusted me enough to tell me their stories about supernatural encounters. I believe you.

The many ghosts who have made my life more fun and exciting.

My guardian angel and spirit guides for their protection and guidance along the way.

Eric Campbell and Lance Wright of Down & Out Books, for being willing to take a chance on publishing a nonfiction book far outside their usual fiction categories.

Dawn Barclay, for her thoughtful copy editing.

My family and friends, who love me despite not always agreeing with me.

Special thanks to my Dad for showing up after death. Love you.

RENEE VALOIS has been an award-winning writer for most of her life, winning a Fellowship in writing from the National Endowment for the Arts, and many national awards for her writing, which has appeared on TV, radio, social media, websites, print magazines and newspapers. For over twelve years, Renee worked for a large international corporation, where she served as Director of Copy. She co-authored a novel, *The Devil and the Diva*, which was one of four finalists for a Minnesota Book Award in genre writing and was named one of the Best Books of the Year by *Minnesota Monthly* magazine.

During Renee's exploration of the spiritual world, she learned from the best, taking classes and workshops from nationally known psychics such as Echo Bodine, Suzanne Giesemann, and Susanne Wilson. She developed a relationship with an amazing ghost psychic and did investigations with well-known TV ghost hunters. Renee frequently encountered earthbound spirits, and during her studies, she learned how to converse with angels and spirit guides.